Investing in India

Founded in 1807, John Wiley & Sons is the oldest independent publishing company in the United States. With offices in North America, Europe, Australia, and Asia, Wiley is globally committed to developing and marketing print and electronic products and services for our customers' professional and personal knowledge and understanding.

The Wiley Finance series contains books written specifically for finance and investment professionals as well as sophisticated individual investors and their financial advisers. Book topics range from portfolio management to e-commerce, risk management, financial engineering, valuation and financial instrument analysis, as well as much more.

For a list of available titles, visit our web site at www.WileyFinance.com.

Investing in India

A Value Investor's Guide to the Biggest Untapped Opportunity in the World

RAHUL SARAOGI

WILEY

Published by John Wiley & Sons, Inc., Hoboken, New Jersey.
Published simultaneously in Canada.

For general information on our other products and services or for technical
support, please contact our Customer Care Department within the United States at
(800) 762-2974, outside the United States at (317) 572-3993 or fax (317) 572-4002.

Wiley publishes in a variety of print and electronic formats and by print-on-
demand. Some material included with standard print versions of this book may
not be included in e-books or in print-on-demand. If this book refers to media
such as a CD or DVD that is not included in the version you purchased, you may
download this material at http://booksupport.wiley.com. For more information
about Wiley products, visit www.wiley.com.

Library of Congress Cataloging-in-Publication Data:

ISBN 9781118756096 (cloth)
ISBN 9781118755945 (ebk)
ISBN 9781118760192 (ebk)

10 9 8 7 6 5 4 3 2 1

For Ruchita and Miraya,
You bring out the best in me.

Contents

Foreword

Steve Sjuggerud
Editor of True Wealth

"**G**et over here to India now," my friend Rahul Saraogi told me in late 2008. "Now is the time to invest."

I went. I was convinced. I invested.

Long story short, I personally pocketed a triple-digit return in Indian stocks in just over a year, following Rahul's advice.

In my decades in the investment business, I have been fortunate to meet many great investors. I think Rahul will become known as one of those great investors.

When we first met at an investment conference in the Caribbean, I was so impressed with Rahul, I kept asking him questions over dinner. In just a few questions, I can tell if a guy doesn't really know what he's doing. But Rahul kept knocking it out of the park with his answers. Impressed, I kept going.

His wife eventually said, "Have you gotten to twenty questions yet?!?" I didn't realize I was quizzing him so intently. He kept saying the right things, and I kept looking for the hole in his story. It didn't exist. He is solid. We became friends.

A few years later (in 2008), Rahul told me it was time to get over to India. I'd never been there before.

Rahul took me around the country to show me some of his favorite investment ideas. We went to a variety of different cities and visited many different businesses. These were incredible businesses, priced dirt cheap. In many cases, Rahul was the only investor that had ever gone to see the company before.

I was impressed. I didn't just put money in India in general ... I actually sent it to Rahul. The triple-digit profit I pocketed was with Rahul's hedge fund.

For me, there is no better person to guide me as a foreigner looking to understand investing in India. You see, Rahul fully understands Indian culture AND American culture. ...

Rahul graduated from an Ivy League school in the United States, fully expecting to find his career in the States. But while in the States, he realized the REAL opportunity was back home in India where he grew up.

He truly understands both places. He also really understands investing. I found this out on Day One (much to the dismay of his wife!), and time with Rahul over the years has confirmed that.

In short, I really can't imagine a better guide than Rahul if you want to understand investing in India.

You are in good hands. ...

Preface

I've wanted to write a book about India for a long time. Persistent encouragement bordering on threats by my business partners, Pratik Sharma and Vedant Mimani, and unwavering support from Laura Walsh and her team at Wiley finally helped me complete the book.

I was born in India into a business family and grew up there. My great grandfather migrated to Burma (now Myanmar) from what is now the Indian state of Haryana in the early twentieth century. He went to Burma as a penniless trader and slowly built up a business in textile trading and pulses processing. He had become the proud owner of an automobile by 1934, the year before my grandfather was born. This, according to my grandfather, was a big event during that time and was a declaration of wealth and prosperity.

My family fled back to India as refugees in 1942 during World War II when the Japanese started bombing British forces in Burma. In 1952, my family moved back to Burma and my grandfather built up a successful business in pharmaceutical trading from scratch. My father was born in Burma in 1955. In 1959, Burma nationalized all assets belonging to foreigners and my family came back to India as refugees for a second time. My grandfather once again built up a business from scratch. This time he saw opportunity in wheat flour milling. He built a successful business that was geographically spread all over India. Things were good for a time. I was born in 1979 into economically happy times in my family. However, by 1987 India had changed its policy of controlled licensing, and the flour milling industry was decimated. In 1989, my father started a readymade garment manufacturing and exporting business. By 2000 he had built a meaningful business and our family saw happy economic times again.

I grew up in an environment where business was discussed almost every night at the dinner table. In my early years, India was still a socialist economy, and my father would tell me stories about America and about its fascinating free market economic system. I was determined to study in the United States, and in 1996, I had the opportunity to pursue my undergraduate education in the United States. I chose to study engineering, at Northwestern University in Evanston, Illinois, because my father and uncle are engineers and I wanted to maintain the family legacy. However, I found myself spending countless hours in the library studying John Maynard Keynes and Ludwig von Mises. My heart was not in engineering, and I transferred to the Wharton School at the University of Pennsylvania in Philadelphia after my first year at Northwestern.

As I studied and learned about economic history, market cycles, and the creation and destruction of wealth, I was fascinated. I discovered that the study of *money* was the key to understanding human society and its evolution. I was no longer interested in any trade or industry and instead became interested in learning how money and markets influenced and determined the fortunes of different industries.

Ironically, while I had gone to the United States to learn about its economic system, the very study got me interested in India's economic history. The study of the U.S. economic system became the backdrop of my study of India's social, political, and economic system. I wanted to find out what had made India one of the richest economies in the world millennia ago and what had transpired during the past 500 years that made India one of the world's poorest countries.

The more I read, the more I spoke to people (including my extended family, friends, and business associates), and the more I studied, the more I discovered.

I realized that there was a huge gap in the understanding of India, its markets, and its economy. I realized that Indians in India, including business owners, financial investors, economists, academics, civil servants, and politicians, were looking at things in silos. They were not looking at things in the context of India's sociology or the value systems, the religious beliefs, and the aspirations of its people. They often had an incomplete understanding of free market systems and what led the United States and western Europe to adopt the systems that they follow today.

I also realized that Western academics, researchers, businesspeople, and investors were clueless about India's history in the context of its economy. I became convinced that there was no way for a Western observer to empathize with and understand India's value systems, compulsions, and aspirations since they had not been immersed in it. My conviction continued to strengthen as I had detailed interactions with second-generation Indian children of immigrant parents in countries like the United States, Dubai, Singapore, and Hong Kong. Although they were born in and lived in Indian families, they had lost contact, context, and the importance of the extended family and the community in India. They were even more confused about India than Indians living in India and Westerners studying or interacting with India.

I am a pure capitalist at heart, and my goal is to succeed and become wealthy in life. I am not ashamed about it and I state it up front. All my study, research, and work had a single motivation—the pursuit of an edge that would help me make more money. My goal was neither to publish academic papers nor to solve the complex socioeconomic problems of the world.

I realized by pure serendipity that the stock market is the best place to learn about and to apply the learning from multiple disciplines. I discovered Warren Buffett, Charlie Munger, and Benjamin Graham (in that order). I spent countless hours reading and learning about everything I could from these investment greats. Through Charlie Munger I discovered Phil Fisher and Robert Cialdini. Through my business partner, Vedant Mimani, I discovered Jesse Livermore and his book *Reminiscences of a Stock Operator* under the pen name Edwin Lefevre. Through Charlie Munger and Phil Fisher I realized the importance of time and the role it plays in determining the success of a good business and the demise of a mediocre business. Through Robert Cialdini and Jesse Livermore I learned the importance of psychology in human decision making and in the markets. About 10 years ago a friend of mine gifted me a copy of Nicholas Nassim Taleb's *Fooled by Randomness*. Taleb validated a lot of things I had learned by practical experience in the markets but had struggled to articulate.

Over the years, I've spoken with my business partners, Vedant and Pratik, about my understanding of India and about the gaps that I believe exist in people's perception and understanding of the country. I've also written many of my thoughts on a blog. However, I had been able to find neither the time nor the motivation to put it all into a structured and organized book.

I've finally managed to complete what I've wanted to do for a long time. This book is a compilation of my understanding of the underlying reality of India from the perspective of a practitioner who has had the privilege of being immersed in two distinct environments and has been able to bridge the knowledge gap between the two.

I hope you enjoy reading this book as much as I have enjoyed writing it.

CHAPTER 1

Understanding India

I ndia is one of the biggest untapped investment opportunities in the world today. However, for many of those investors who have tried to participate in the India story in recent times, the experience has been one of disappointment. Some of the disappointment has been caused by the fact that India has been in the midst of very large transitions in its economy, society as well as politics during the past two decades and the rest of it has been caused by the lack of sufficient understanding of India on the part of investors themselves. Before we explore the challenges and investment opportunities that India presents, it is important to understand where India and Indians are coming from.

AGRARIAN ROOTS

India is one of the great civilizations of the world. Almost everything about India can be linked back to its agrarian roots. India is one of the unique regions of the world that is called a subcontinent.

The mighty Himalayas together with the Tibetan plateau, often referred to as the roof of the world, cut India off from the rest of the northern hemisphere and create a subcontinent that is one of the most fertile agricultural regions on the planet. Like Egypt is called the gift of the Nile, India can be called the gift of the Himalayas. From the north, the Himalayas cut off the subcontinent from the cold Siberian winds that ravage the rest of China and central Asia during the winter. From the south, the Himalayas act as a wall that forces the moisture-laden southwest monsoon winds to precipitate on the subcontinent. The Himalayas act as such a formidable barrier that they force the winds to turn back south and continue precipitation on the subcontinent as the retreating northeast monsoon winds.

The snow-capped Himalayas are the source of perennial rivers that are the lifelines of the great plains of India. The Indus, the Ganges, the Yamuna, and the Brahmaputra all have their sources in the Himalayas.

One statistic can quantify the fertility of India's landmass. About 46 percent of India's landmass is cultivable compared to 18 percent for the United States and only 13 percent for China.

Geopolitically, the Himalayas together with the Indus in the west and the Brahmaputra in the east create formidable natural barriers that kept away many invaders from India for millennia.

To understand India, one needs to understand the role that family, community, religion, and spirituality play in the lives of Indians. And to understand these, one needs to understand India's agrarian roots and India's villages.

INDIA'S VILLAGES

It is often said about Americans that they are among the most insular and provincial people in the world. Fewer than 30 percent of Americans have passports and even fewer have traveled overseas. Foreign visitors often mock what is considered *news* on American television. For most Americans war is no different from a television show. Prior to 9/11, the only modern warfare experienced by the United States on its soil was the attack on Pearl Harbor during World War II and even then it was on the remote islands of Hawaii.

One cannot blame Americans for being the way they are. It is a country that spans an entire continent from west to east. The United States' soil is so naturally rich and its economic system so powerful that most people can enjoy a very high standard of living no matter where they live in the country. India is no different from the United States, and inhabitants of Indian villages are no different from Americans in that context.

India's landmass is so fertile and India's climate is so conducive to the survival of people and domesticated animals that villages in India have been self-sufficient in whatever they needed for millennia. The relative security provided by India's natural geographic boundaries, left its villages insular and undisturbed for centuries. The self-sufficiency of Indian villages left India open to political invasions over the centuries. Indians did not care who crowned himself king and who ruled the country as long as the basic fabric of village life was left undisturbed.

What is fascinating about India is that despite being ruled by Muslim rulers for eight centuries and by Christian rulers for two centuries, 80 percent of Indians are still Hindu. This illustrates how tightly knit the fabric of India's village society is.

With basic survival not a concern, India's village society over millennia and centuries evolved practices, rituals, and beliefs that perpetuated their desired way of life and made the system so rigid that nothing could dislodge it.

THE ROLE OF THE FAMILY

India is a paternalistic society. In villages, agricultural land belongs to the family or the patriarch and is passed down to sons over generations. Sons and their families live together with their parents in the same house and work together on the family farm. Women are usually responsible for the cattle and dairy farm together with raising the family and taking care of the household.

In northern India, at the time of marriage, the girl leaves her parents' house behind and moves into her husband's *joint family* house. The girl severs all economic ties with her parents and brothers at the time of marriage. At the time of marriage, the girl brings with her a *dowry* from her parents' home to her husband's home. Many different theories exist to explain the origins of the concept of dowry. One theory that resonates with a large number of people is the idea that since the girl severs economic ties with her parents and brothers, she takes her economic interest in the joint family with her to her husband's household as dowry. This practice has become very corrupted over centuries and has put girls, especially in poor households, in such hardship that the government of India has banned the practice by law. Dowry, however, remains widely accepted and practiced throughout India.

Weddings play a very important role in Indian villages. It is almost always considered a marriage of two families. In some tightly knit communities, it is even considered a marriage of two villages. In times past, weddings would last for weeks and all members of the village would work together to welcome their guests from the other village for the wedding and would participate in the celebrations and festivities.

SEVEN GENERATIONS

Given that village life was quite stable, static, and did not change much from generation to generation, the concept of lineage and family name became very strong. If one is successful in one's ventures, it is believed in India (and often true) that one's seven succeeding generations live well and prosper. The reverse is true as well. Debts in Indian villages are not forgiven at death and are considered the burden of successive generations. It is believed that if one fails in one's ventures, then the burden of the misfortune haunts one's seven succeeding generations.

Family name and reputation became a strong anchor in India's value system. Feuds between families and associated revenge across multiple generations became part of folklore.

Property rights and property ownership became closely integrated into the fabric of the Indian family system. Since property continued to be owned by families through multiple generations, the title and ownership of property was conventionally associated with family and family name. Confiscation of property by the crown or the state was not possible, and the entire village system would rally behind such blasphemy.

Indians in villages lived in joint families and sacrificed many of their independent freedoms to fulfill the wishes of their elders. The unwritten rule of the joint family system was that one's children would do for one what he or she did for his or her parents. Elders provided support, stability, and counsel to their younger generation, and the younger generation cared for their elders in their years of need.

Given that families shared joint fortunes, getting one's son settled in work or business was the equivalent of investing in a pension plan or investing for retirement for most fathers. And caring for one's elders, especially in sickness and old age, was a very important attribute of the Indian value system.

There is a popular joke about the Indian farmer who is toiling away on his field in the hot sun when he hears the news about the birth of his son. On hearing the news, he puts away his implements and decides to sleep under a shady tree. A passerby asks him why he is not working and he replies that he no longer needs to; he says that he is the proud father of a son and his son will now carry his burden.

Sibling rivalry is also a historically well-documented attribute of the Indian joint family system. Families in their unity would routinely shield the incompetent members of the family, and the competent members would carry the burden of the entire family. Occasionally, the competent sibling would challenge the burden of the incompetent one and families would break apart. Indian folklore sympathizes with the underdog, and popular opinion always divides individuals into two categories: the incompetent and kind sibling, and the competent and callous sibling.

Sustaining the joint family system is becoming difficult in modern India. As India urbanizes, the joint family system is breaking down. Since incomes in urban areas are often the outcome of individual effort and not derived from a family estate, cross-subsidization of nonperforming members of the family is often unacceptable and results in family splits. Cost of housing in urban areas also makes it hard to build and live in large dwellings that can accommodate a joint family. Joint families in urban areas have therefore become the privilege of the rich.

As Indians become more educated and experience demand for their talent from around the world, families have started splintering. One very frequently finds elderly couples with empty nests living in urban India, while their offspring study or work and live abroad. Parents seldom wish to follow their children and usually prefer staying behind in familiar surroundings.

CASE STUDY: The Saga of the Ambani Brothers

One of the most spectacular family splits of recent times was that of brothers Mukesh Ambani and Anil Ambani of the Reliance Group that broke into the open in November 2004. The feud had been simmering in private since the death of their father and patriarch, Dhirubhai Ambani, in July 2002.

Reliance Industries Limited (RIL: IN) at the time was among India's top five companies ranked by market capitalization as well as profitability. The publicly fought battles between siblings had significant relevance to financial markets as millions of minority shareholders, including institutional investors from India and outside India, were impacted by the mudslinging and media battles fought by the brothers. It took the intervention of no less than the finance minister of the country to sort out issues between the brothers and to help them arrive at a workable settlement.

What amazed observers was that assets worth billions of dollars changed title between siblings and not a dime in taxes (estate, wealth, capital gains, or income) was paid in the process.

The feud lasted for several months in the public domain, and an official settlement was reached only in August 2005. Several large investors exited their investments in stocks of companies belonging to the group during this time. Some were genuinely concerned about the potential value destruction that would take place in companies of the group as a result of the public feud, and some others were disgusted by the blatant disregard for corporate governance and minority shareholder interests that was exhibited.

However, for those who understood India and understood the motivations behind the feud, the feud itself was the biggest reason to invest in companies of the group. The brothers were fighting (at least apparently) over different points of view related to unlocking of value in companies that were embedded inside Reliance Industries.

The messy process aside, there were a few bets that one could easily make. First, there was unlikely to be any value destruction in the process, as both brothers were focused value creators. Second, having gone down the path they did, a split was inevitable and likely to be reached sooner rather than later. Family splits in India have happened for centuries and are par for the course. Third, whatever the eventual split combination, the sum of the parts that emerged was likely to be greater than the whole that existed presplit.

It turned out that the demerger of the subsidiary companies from Reliance Industries was one of the biggest value-unlocking events in the history of corporate India. In November 2004, Reliance Industries stock traded around INR550 per share. By August 2005, when the split was formally announced, the stock had moved up to INR750 per share. Shareholders who weathered the uncertainty surrounding the family drama were rewarded for their patience. However, even for those investors who bought the stock once the split was announced, the family settlement created tremendous value.

The demerger was completed in February 2006 and by April 2006 the value of the shares of Reliance Industries and the market value of the shares of the demerged companies that were given to Reliance Industries shareholders aggregated INR 1,300 per share.

Events that might have concerned distant observers became big value-creating opportunities for investors who truly understood the motivations behind India's family systems.

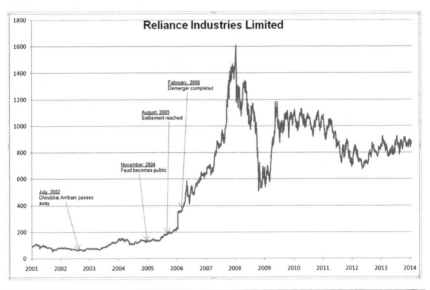

COLONIALISM AND ITS IMPACT ON INDIAN VILLAGES

The British came to India as traders. They were surprised at the ease with which they were able to divide and conquer India's small and prosperous princely states. The English East India Company became one of the earliest corporations in the world to have a standing army. It wasn't until the armed mutiny of 1857 that the British Crown took over the administration of India.

The British were great administrators. While they were able to overthrow rulers and bring the entire country under the British Crown, the rigidity of India's village systems frustrated them and posed immense challenges. They were able to shake up the system in some places and miserably failed in several others.

They surveyed the entire country and established undisputable land records and titles that had not existed before. They also created a land-owning *noble* class called *zamindars* that were endowed with the ownership and administration of large parcels of land often spanning several villages. This made the villagers landless laborers and created tremendous resentment among them.

Land has been a very sensitive subject in India for millennia. Since villages were insular and subsistence oriented, the importance of land in village life was immeasurable. Alienating one from one's land was probably the biggest punishment one could give an individual and his family and most often resulted in destitution and abject poverty for them.

In fact, land redistribution among landless farm laborers was one of the big reform activities undertaken immediately after independence by the government of India. However, the government wasn't able to do enough. The eastern part of India with the state of West Bengal at its center was at the heart of the zamindari movement in British India. It was here in a tiny village called Naxalbari that Marxist revolutionaries started armed agitation for land redistribution among landless labor. The movement was called the *naxalite* movement and gave birth to the Communist Party of India. The movement has since morphed and has become a big menace for law and order in India.

CASE STUDY: Tata Motors and the Singur Protest Movement

When Tata Motors (TTMT: IN) announced the Tata Nano in 2006 as the middle-class Indian's entry-level car with a previously unthinkable price tag of US$2,500, the company's chairman Ratan Tata and stories of frugal Indian engineering made it to the cover of every business and engineering magazine around the world. The Tata Nano was hailed as the innovation of the year in 2006 and in 2008 *Time* magazine named it among The Dozen Most Important Cars of All Time.

However, by 2011, *Time* had written an article about the Tata Nano titled "The Little Car That Couldn't." Behind this dramatic turn of events was one of India's most infamous land protest movements, centered in the tiny village of Singur in the Indian state of West Bengal.

West Bengal is one of India's poorest states and one of its least industrialized. Ratan Tata had wanted to play the role of benevolent captain of Indian industry and had decided to *gift* the Tata Nano project to the state of West Bengal. For its part, the state government had rolled out the red carpet for the company and for its army of component suppliers and subcontractors.

The site chosen was the village of Singur on the outskirts of the city of Kolkata (previously known as Calcutta). By his own admission, Ratan Tata had highlighted that Singur was an inhospitable area to locate a mega car factory. Like much of the state of West Bengal, Singur was flooded under water for half the year and the level of the land had to be raised significantly and at great expense to enable the construction of the factory complex.

However, within a few months of the nomination of Singur as the site for the Tata Nano plant, the village erupted into protests against the setting up of the car factory. At first, it seemed like expected clamoring by villagers for higher compensation for their acquired land. But the protests refused to die down. In fact, within a short time, the protests became so heated that it brought in the involvement of the political opposition in the state. The issue became a media circus and baffled India and the rest of the world. No one was able to understand why the people of the region were protesting against one of the biggest employment-generating opportunities to come their way in decades. Only 1,500 farmers were affected by the dislocation, and their land was being cropped only once per year compared to three times a year elsewhere in West Bengal. One could clearly see that the potential employment that would be generated from the factory would far exceed any loss of farm livelihood.

The government of West Bengal used the archaic 1894 imperial law called *eminent domain* to acquire land in Singur to hand over to the Tatas and did it in a forceful manner. This touched a raw nerve in the population of Singur and the state of West Bengal. The poor and illiterate farmers of this sleepy village were willing to fight to any extent and were willing to sacrifice all future employment and prosperity opportunities in order to safeguard the right to their land and to their property. To them, it was not an issue about economic benefits and development but rather one about their individual freedom and their rights to their property.

Tata Motors subsequently decided to shift its mega factory from Singur to the Indian state of Gujarat. The Singur episode doomed the Tata Nano, and Tata Motors and its suppliers incurred significant losses in the entire process. Tata Motors' stock price declined from INR180 in early 2006 to INR80 in September 2008, even before the Lehman Brothers crisis erupted. By the end of 2008, the stock was down to INR30 and had fallen by 84 percent since the announcement of the Nano project.

People took away different messages from the happenings in Singur. Foreign investors looked at the drama wearily and wondered what chance they stood of investing in India if one of India's most respected business houses had faced such trouble in making a transformational investment. The events no doubt cast a long shadow on India's credentials as an investment destination. In my opinion, they failed to pay sufficient heed to the underlying reality behind the events at Singur.

However, my bigger takeaway from the Singur protest movement was that of the sanctity of property rights in India. The protests clearly demonstrated that property rights in India are inviolable. No government or private party can forcibly steal property that rightfully belongs to someone else in India—at least not *en masse*. This single fact gives me tremendous comfort as an investor in India.

The British also established a strong judicial system with a civil and criminal code based on English common law. While in earlier times disputes in each village were resolved by the elders of the village based on traditions and beliefs of that particular village, the establishment of a uniform code gave people a chance at natural justice. This did not go down well with the rigid Indian village system either. The British rulers succeeded in a limited way in enforcing the criminal code; however, in civil matters, the individual decisions of the village governing council continued to reign supreme.

In the India that emerged post-independence, land titles, together with an independent judiciary, for the first time empowered landowners in villages and gave them the ability to trade their property and to leave their village for a life in cities that were being newly built.

Although the process was slow, the changes had slowly but surely started altering the status quo that had existed in India for centuries.

DEEP-ROOTED BELIEFS AND ASPIRATIONS

It is often said that one can take the boy out of the village, but it is very difficult to take the village out of the boy. The story of the belief systems and aspirations of Indians is somewhat similar. After centuries of having nurtured value systems that sustained village life, Indians, even those who live in urban areas, have deep-rooted beliefs and aspirations that resonate with their past. While urbanization has affected these belief systems in significant ways, in many ways the belief systems have remained the same.

For investors, it is very important to understand these belief systems in order to understand why things happen the way they do and in order to make better-informed guesses about future outcomes.

Affinity for Land

Having lived in agrarian villages for millennia in rigid joint families and having survived on subsistence agriculture, people in India realized at a very deep level the importance of owning land. Every family owned and was expected to own land in the village, which was cultivated by them and was the source of the family's livelihood. Land was not only a source of income and livelihood but also an insurance policy against unforeseen difficult times. One of the manifestations of difficult times was when a family was forced to sell its land for extraordinary circumstances. The family was then considered *bhumiheen,* or landless. Being bhumiheen was considered a big stigma in Indian villages.

If a son sold his family's land to pay for his misadventures or to provide capital for a venture, his father would chide him that he had made his father bhumiheen. This was a big burden on the son and a big source of grief for the father.

This affinity for owning land manifests itself in interesting ways among urban Indians. While in most parts of the world, land is treated as the raw material for building a usable real asset like a home or a commercial building, in India, a large part of the time, land is treated as a *consumption* item that provides its buyer satisfaction in ownership, never to be used for any purpose whatsoever. Urban Indians, without regard to their income level and wealth, exhibit a strong desire to own vacant land. This desire to own vacant land is in addition to their desire to own a home to live in.

Driving along highways in India, one often finds *developments* that are nothing more than large parcels of land that have been plotted into smaller housing lots with internal roads and basic infrastructure built out. While these are often marketed as potential housing sites, their strange locations with large distances from existing inhabitation clearly give away the fact that their buyers have no intention of building homes there for a long time to come. Developers of these sites create projects that serve all income strata of Indians. It does not hurt that large amounts of unaccounted or *black money* is used in land transactions and that it permits individuals to stash away their illegal income as savings for the future (more about that later). The wealthiest Indians, for their part, tend to own vacant parcels of land in prime locations in Indian cities without any intention of selling or developing them.

The ownership of land for consumption distorts the market for homebuyers on the fringes. One often hears people complain that homes in India are unaffordable for the average Indian and that home prices are far higher than affordability based on income levels would suggest. Observers have warned of *bubbles* in Indian land prices for decades. The warnings have become especially loud in recent times.

In my opinion, there is no bubble in land prices in India. This is because there is no leverage used in the purchase of land. The Reserve Bank of India prohibits banks and financial institutions from making loans against and for the purchase of vacant land. I agree that a certain amount of concealed leverage does find its way into the land market, but the amounts are not alarming or significant.

Since India is a rapidly urbanizing and a very populated country, land has been a rewarding asset to own. This has further reinforced the affinity for land among urban Indians and has validated the beliefs passed down by their family elders. It will take an elongated period of disappointment with owning land to even make a marginal dent in their affinity.

Homeownership

There is an old Tamil saying that *one is not a man until he has built his house and married his daughter*. The desire for homeownership is very deeply entrenched in the Indian psyche. Living in a rented home is a source of great dissatisfaction for the average Indian. It would not be a stretch to say that the average Indian derives a great source of joy and satisfaction that exceeds the marginal utility of shelter in owning a home.

When one looks at home prices in major Indian urban areas, one is often perplexed about how average Indians can afford them. The nonaffordability of homes based on conventional metrics exists not just in the prime and the most expensive areas of cities, but extends all the way to their peripheries. The immediate reaction of the casual observer is that real estate prices are in a bubble and need to correct in a meaningful way. However, the disparity between home prices and income levels has existed in Indian cities for decades and is increasing rather than decreasing.

The reason the disparity exists is that buying a home is a family project and not just an individual project in India. In the southern part of India, parents will often gift a home to their daughter as a wedding present, in which she will most likely not live and will most likely rent out for extra income. It is not uncommon for parents, uncles, aunts, siblings, in-laws, or close friends to help young couples bridge affordability shortfalls in their quest for homeownership. While homes are the largest asset owned by average Americans, for average Indians, their home is probably the *only* asset owned by them (other than the gold jewelry owned by the woman of the house).

Nepotism and Dynasty

India has no estate taxes. The very basis of the Indian family system can be summarized by the Swiss watch company Patek Phillipe's tag line: *You never actually own it. You merely look after it for the next generation.* It is essential for investors to understand this deep-rooted belief in the Indian psyche to make better-informed decisions.

Succession and how leadership changes from one generation to the next is the subject of folklore in India. Epics like the *Ramayana* and *Mahabharata*, written centuries ago, are the equivalent of modern-day soap operas and are anchored around the succession struggles of princely kingdoms. The debate about whether leadership should transition to the eldest or to the most competent son in the next generation has been around in India from before the time these epics were written.

Indians subconsciously accept transfer of power, both economic and political, by lineage and dynasty. Meritocracy is a Western concept that has gained acceptance in recent decades and remains a mostly urban phenomenon that is not very widespread. The nepotism inherent in the Indian psyche is clearly manifested in the visible sense of entitlement demonstrated by young adult boys from successful political and business families. Even those boys who have been educated at top Western universities and have been immersed in a meritocratic environment for extended periods will often justify their sense of entitlement with the retort that the family's assets have been passed down for generations and do not necessarily belong to the previous generation.

This nepotistic mind-set creates problems in modern-day public corporations with millions of minority shareholders. Competent professional managers struggle to work in cohesion with significantly less competent crown princes who often get involved in management. Many professional managers leave during times of such transitions, and others watch their companies decline to mediocrity and often into oblivion.

CASE STUDY: Ranbaxy: The Indian Pharmaceutical Multinational

Ranbaxy Laboratories Limited (RBXY: IN) is the ultimate tale of Indian entrepreneurship. It is a story of inspiration that has ignited a million dreams. The company was bought from its original founders by Bhai Mohan Singh in 1952. But the real story of Ranbaxy started when Bhai Mohan Singh's son, Parvinder Singh, joined the company in 1967. Parvinder Singh was more like a first-generation entrepreneur than an inheritor.

From humble beginnings as an importer of pharmaceutical products, Ranbaxy morphed into a branded formulations company that sold drugs under license from foreign owners. In time, Ranbaxy added generic drugs to its product portfolio, and during the past 15 years has become one of the largest exporters of pharmaceutical products from India.

Ranbaxy's market value at the time it went public in 1973 was US$50,000 converted from Indian rupees to U.S. dollars at today's exchange rate. In 2008, the company was sold to Daiichi Sankyo of Japan for a market value of US$4.6 billion.

The Ranbaxy journey was interrupted when the patriarch, Parvinder Singh, died suddenly in 1999. Parvinder Singh's sons, Malvinder and Shivinder, were too young and inexperienced to take over the business, and the reins went to D. S. Brar, who was a professional handpicked by Parvinder Singh himself. Under D. S. Brar, Ranbaxy went from strength to strength. However, the cancer of nepotism was festering under the hood. In 2004, D. S. Brar left the company, and Malvinder Singh was inducted into the board of the company as president of the pharmaceuticals division. Brian Tempest, who was loyal to the Singh's and was a temporary placeholder, took over the role of CEO and managing director. In 2006, Tempest handed over the reins to Malvinder Singh and took on a board supervisory role.

Under Malvinder Singh, and even before that under Brian Tempest, the company started heading down a path it should not have gone and the company lost its culture and ethos. The culture of straight dealing was replaced by a culture of misdealing and lies. In 2008, Malvinder Singh managed to sell Ranbaxy to Japanese pharmaceutical company Daiichi Sankyo at an inflated valuation with misrepresentations galore. What Daiichi Sankyo realized soon after taking over Ranbaxy was that they had been told white lies and that the company was in much worse shape than they had anticipated. They felt cheated, and India's reputation of fair dealing in the eyes of both the Japanese and the rest of the world took a major hit.

When Parvinder Singh died in July 1999, Ranbaxy's stock price was INR210 (adjusted for splits), and in 2004 when D. S. Brar quit the company, its stock price had more than doubled to INR475. However, the stock languished for the next few years under Brian Tempest and Malvinder Singh and was still at INR475 in June 2008 four years later when Daiichi Sankyo bought the company. Malvinder Singh sold the company to Daiichi Sankyo in June 2008 for INR737 per share in what was nothing short of a shenanigan. By March 2009, the stock had fallen to INR135 (partially because of the global financial meltdown), a price that was closer to the underlying reality of the company.

The big takeaway here is that the Daiichi Sankyo deal was an aberration caused by the euphoria surrounding the India story at the time and probably never should have happened. Under normal circumstances, the stock price would have converged to the underlying reality of the business, and that reality was downright ugly. The mismanagement of one of India's blue-chip companies by the incompetent heirs of the all-star entrepreneur Parvinder Singh had destroyed almost all the value that had been created by him and his team by their hard work and focus over decades.

The impact of generational transitions is visible not just in governance but in capital allocation as well. Since there are no estate taxes in India, wealth accumulates very rapidly in families. Once a family's business becomes a certain size, let's say $200 million in market capitalization, a sense of contentment often sets in. If the family owns half the business, the net worth of the family becomes $100 million. While $100 million is a lot of money anywhere in the world, in India, with its tightly knit family support systems and no estate taxes, it is a very large amount of money. The motivations of the family then start to change.

Some start to get politically involved, while others get drawn to the glitz and glamour of the entertainment industry. Many others might be drawn toward spirituality and social good. Contrary to what one would believe, most Indian families *do not* aspire to become mega-rich and do not aspire to appear on wealth league tables. A majority of families value preserving their customs, traditions, and way of life above all else. Protecting the weak and the incompetent and propping them up to keep the family together is valued more than growth and progress.

The net outcome of this mind-set is that in a large number of cases, mediocrity becomes pervasive in the family and in the business and the return on capital if the business crashes. This is a terrible outcome for minority shareholders but is one that repeats itself periodically and consistently.

Delusional investors often point to illustrious track records of the previous generations and fail to take into account the changed future trajectory of the business.

The good news here is that the rise of companies founded by professionals and first-generation technocrats often backed by venture capital and private equity is rapidly changing the landscape. Not only do these professionally managed companies protect minority shareholders better, but they also serve as role models for first-generation entrepreneurs who now realize that it is no longer necessary to be a part of the old boys' club of dynastic wealth to be successful in business in India.

The key takeaway from the discussion on nepotism and dynasty is that investors need to look at the people and families behind the businesses they seek to invest in very closely while evaluating investments in India.

SPIRITUALITY AND SUPERSTITION

No study of India and its value systems can be complete without an appreciation and understanding of the role that spirituality and superstition plays in the lives of average Indians.

Hinduism is considered one the most tolerant religions in the world, recent fundamentalist uprisings notwithstanding. The reason is that Hinduism is not even a religion in the conventional sense. It can be described as a way of life or the collection of practices and beliefs of people that inhabit the subcontinent to the south of the river Indus, referred to historically as Hindustan (derived from Indus). Hinduism does not have a unified theology and does not have a unified sacred doctrine or text. When the British needed a Hindu sacred text to administer corporal oaths before depositions in the court of law, they picked the Bhagavad Gita in the absence of a unified text. However, a very large number of people who consider themselves Hindu, especially those who call themselves Shaivites (or followers of Lord Shiva) do not necessarily revere the Bhagavad Gita.

Followers of Vedanta Hinduism refer to the Vedas or the Upanishads as their sacred doctrine, and according to them, epics like the *Ramayana* and *Mahabharata* are mere commentaries in the evolution of vedantic thought. However, Vaishnavites, or followers of Lord Vishnu, refer to these epics as real-life recordings of the most significant *avatars* of Lord Vishnu. While Jains, followers of Lord Mahavira, and Buddhists, followers of Lord Buddha, disassociate themselves from Hinduism completely, Hindus liberally justify away the existence of these spiritual teachers as avatars of Lord Vishnu.

The purpose of the preceding illustration is not to get mired in philosophical or theological debate or discussion, as that is not the goal of this book. The purpose of the illustration is to merely provide a peek into the myriad beliefs and practices that remain in existence in India in contradiction with each other. India has truly been a land of spiritual experimentation over millennia. Experimentation has been allowed to flourish through the ages by the sustenance capacity of the soil and the climate.

Despite the onset of modern medicine, technology, and communication, Indians remain a population mired in superstition and blind faith. Higher education and increased wealth and prosperity do not seem to have diminished this and, in many cases, seem to have accentuated it. Because India has historically been a trading nation, and commerce has formed the backbone of the Indian civilization for a very long time, Indians are well versed with the vagaries of chance and fortune. Their attempts at taming an essentially untamable and impermanent world have created and sustained a large industry in spirituality and rites and rituals over the ages. In the modern day of satellite television and the Internet, this industry continues to prosper and thrive. India remains a big market for Godmen of all kinds, fortune tellers, astrologers, and their morphed brethren numerologists and *vaastu* (similar to Chinese *feng-shui*) consultants. Their clientele span the entire spectrum, from the very poor to the very rich and the completely illiterate to the highly educated. They bind society and civilization in a cloak of morality and piety. Indians often refer to the pious among them as *god-fearing* individuals.

The fortunes of the Tirumala Venkateswara temple (estimated at US$10 billion) and the recently valued treasures of the Sree Padmanabhaswamy temple (estimated at US$18 billion) in southern India are manifestations of the importance attached to spirituality in India by royal families and businesspeople over the ages. Legend has it that Lord Venkateswara of the Tirumala Venkateswara temple borrowed money from Lord Kubera, the divine treasurer, for his wedding to Goddess Padmavathi and promised to repay the loan with interest with the help of his devotees. Popular belief is that Lord Venkateswara is still servicing the interest on the debt and the principal remains unpaid. Devotees and followers believe that helping Lord Venkateswara repay his debts to Lord Kubera is a meritorious deed and results in good fortune. They often make Lord Venkateswara a partner in their businesses and diligently deposit his share of profits from their businesses into the temple trust.

Understanding the spiritual and superstitious psyche of Indians is essential to successfully investing in India. This is because the manifestations of these beliefs appear in the Indian economy in the most unexpected (for the uninitiated) of places. Indians often prefer investing in big-ticket items like property and machinery only during certain auspicious times of the year, and often avoid such investments altogether during certain other times of the year. Weddings—which are a big driver of the Indian economy, given its young demographic—are scheduled only during certain times of the year and are avoided during certain other times, making them a seasonal activity. This can have a significant impact on availability and pricing of things like hotels, catering, and allied services. In many parts of the country, especially in the south, houses and buildings that are not built according to *vaastu* often sell at significant discounts to market prices due to their believed propensity to bring misfortune to the owner.

Many times, investors are confounded by strange behavior on the part of individuals in government or in corporations. Infrequently, potential business deals get scuttled and potential employees behave in unpredictable ways without apparent reason. There is usually a reason for such behavior, and it often lies in some spiritual or metaphysical belief that drives individuals to behave in those ways.

Urbanization is changing some of these quirks but is reinforcing several others. It is safe to assume that Indians do not always behave in the most rational ways and that they maintain a strong link with spirituality and superstition.

VILLAGES ARE NOT THE SAME ANYMORE

Two things happened that completely shook up the foundation of Indian village life. The first was the industrial revolution and its evolved offspring called globalization. The second was the communication revolution, which through satellite television, mobile phones, and the Internet brought knowledge about the fruits of industrialization and globalization into every village home.

One's sense of well-being is relative. In a closed village system where almost everyone is equally poor, people become content with their lot in life and are often not able to visualize upward mobility. However, with the world visible on their television screens, people (especially youth) in villages started to aspire for a better life. They realized quickly that the land would not be able to provide sufficient income to meet their aspirations and that their only hope was to migrate to urban areas.

For rural Indians who migrated to urban areas, the experience has not been all hunky-dory. A vast majority of them found themselves working in menial jobs and in jobs like construction that required hard labor. The story of urban India is one of sprawling shanties and slums with living conditions no better than those that these migrants left behind in their poor villages.

However, the big game changer has been education. As the telecom and Internet revolution connected India's villages to its cities, it also connected India to the developed world. The arbitrage between low-priced and high-skilled talent in India and similar talent in the developed world gave rise to India's information technology (IT) services industry. For those rural migrants who managed to educate themselves, the IT services industry provided a life and standard of living that could never have been imagined by those back in the villages they left behind. While the IT industry employed only a few million people, it kindled the dreams and ambitions of hundreds of millions of parents and their children.

The aspiration for a better life away from the land and the desire to achieve it through access to better education has ignited an exodus out of Indian villages. The Indian census of 2011 recorded that 31 percent of India's population of 1.20 billion people lived in what are classified as semiurban or urban areas. It is expected that by 2031, 50 percent of India's population will live in semiurban or urban areas. This will mean a doubling of the population of already crowded Indian cities and will probably require the building of several new ones.

The trend of rural to urban migration in India is an inevitability whose time has come. I cannot fathom any scenario that might cause a reversal of this trend. The migration is throwing up numerous opportunities just as it creates numerous challenges in its wake.

URBANIZATION IS CHANGING INDIA

In the rigid village structure where everyone knows everyone else and where families and bloodlines become branded and bucketed for events, achievements, and failures in bygone eras, it becomes very difficult for individuals and families to get a clean start.

Urban India offers individuals and families the hope of a fresh start with the complete anonymity it forces upon them. What matters in crowded and expensive urban India is the work and effort that one does in the present. It does not matter where one is coming from or what one has achieved in the past. It is the great equalizer and leveler for those without anything and those coming from the bottom-most rungs of class and caste structures in villages. In urban India, each individual's fortunes are tied to where he or she is headed and not where he or she is coming from. This is a complete break from the way things were for most Indians in the bygone eras, and its significance cannot be overemphasized.

While urban India brings with it tremendous upward mobility, it also breaks down what are considered traditional Indian value systems like the ones discussed earlier.

The biggest driver of urbanization, however, remains education. As discussed earlier, the belief that higher education leads to a better standard of living has been indelibly imprinted in the Indian psyche. Even though commentators often point to the poor quality of Indian higher education (on average) and the lack of benchmarking to global standards, the availability of this mediocre quality education in urban agglomerations far surpasses anything available in Indian villages. Education has become the great leveler of the infamous Indian hierarchical class and caste system.

SUMMARY

Understanding India and the motivations and aspirations of Indians is very important for successfully investing in India. In my experience of investing in the Indian public markets, I have seen investors approach the markets in a very top-down manner with a Western or global framework and fail miserably. They suffer from the syndrome of the man with a hammer looking for nails.

Investors often get carried away by sectoral themes like *infrastructure* or *outsourcing* or *domestic demand* and fail to look at the motivations of people. They misunderstand and wrongly extrapolate likely consumer behavior and build erroneous models. They fail to sufficiently evaluate the people who manage and control corporations and fail to recognize what drives them.

Conversely, investors often miss opportunities that are unique to India. The fact that something has not worked elsewhere in the world does not mean that it will not necessarily work in India. Understanding the idiosyncrasies of the Indian population can often provide clues to investments that can be significant return generators over time.

India is by no means a static country, and the dynamism of change is visible even to the casual first-time visitor to the country. While India is a very old civilization and has deep-rooted beliefs and traditions, it is also a very young country that is changing and embracing the new very rapidly. The great hope for the economic future of India is its large population, young demographic, rapid rate of urbanization, and rapidly rising skill sets and education levels of its youth.

CHAPTER 2

Government, Politics, and the Media

India is a complex country. It is the largest democracy in the world. It is a frustrating country to deal with whether in the context of business, diplomacy, or geopolitics. Investors and commentators often jump to negative conclusions and generate negative forecasts about the future of India due to the confusing nature of its politics and governance. India has often been compared to a slow-moving elephant, whereas some of its more aggressive and agile peers have been compared to tigers. However, the very form of government that has frustrated investors is India's biggest strength. It is this very form of government that is likely to make India one of the biggest investment success stories of this century.

IS INDIA ONE COUNTRY?

In 2009, a white paper published on the web site of the China International Institute of Strategic Studies in Beijing referred to India as a string of pearls and suggested that the Chinese government should break India into a number of smaller pieces by supporting its ethnic divisions and its neighbors. It also suggested that historically, India was never one country.

India has 28 states divided on a linguistic basis and seven union territories administered by the national government. While the *national* language of India is Hindi, most people outside the central plains do not speak it. The British unified India and made it into a single country. Even just prior to independence in 1947, undivided India had 562 princely states (erstwhile kingdoms) that were protectorates of the British. The British used English as the language of business, law, and government, and it has continued to this day. They built a robust civil service and bureaucracy that brought uniform administration to the entire country. Indians from different parts of the country are able to communicate with each other because of the widespread use of English.

One wonders why Nepal and Bhutan are not a part of India when Sikkim and Meghalaya are a part of India. One wonders why Sri Lanka is not a part of India when Kerala is a part of India. Burma (now Myanmar) was ruled by the British from Delhi until 1937. Why is Burma not a part of India when Nagaland and Mizoram are a part of India? Why are the Maldives not a part of India when the Lakshadweep Islands and the Andaman and Nicobar Islands are a part of India?

India has more Muslims than Pakistan, but Pakistan is an independent Islamic republic. People in India's Punjab state speak the same Punjabi language and practice the same type of farming irrigated by the same river system as the people in Pakistan's Punjab province. However, people in India's Punjab state and India's Kerala states that have almost nothing in common are part of the same country, whereas the people of Indian Punjab and Pakistani Punjab are divided by an international border.

What I am trying to get at here is that the sovereign borders of India are an accident of history and geopolitics and not the outcome of a natural historical union of peoples.

However, as hard to believe and as fascinating as it is, India *is* one country. Even though it has a federal system of government like the United States, it is not a union of independent nations and peoples like the European Union. The people of the Indian subcontinent have been unified repeatedly throughout history. India was first unified by religion and philosophy (Buddhism, Jainism, Hinduism), then by invasion (Muslim rulers, Europeans), then by administration (British), and finally by democracy.

Emperor Ashoka was the first ruler to unify India in 260 B.C. He unified India by force and conquest and then spread the teachings of the Buddha throughout the length and breadth of the subcontinent and beyond to foreign lands.

The earliest Muslim rulers invaded India in the eleventh century. Mughal Emperor Akbar once again unified the country in sixteenth century by force and ruled over it for 50 years. The Europeans came to India as traders between A.D. 1500 and 1600 and found a fragmented country that they could easily conquer by dividing its people and making them fight with each other.

The British ruled India for 200 years, with their first conquest of Indian territory in A.D. 1750. They consolidated and unified India under the British crown in A.D. 1858. The British built the steel frame of India's civil service. They connected the country by railways. They surveyed and mapped the entire country and put in place a legal system based on English common law and natural justice.

The amazing thing about India is that despite being ruled by Muslim and Christian rulers, whose mission was to convert the population to their faith, for over 1,000 years, 80 percent of India's population is still Hindu. I believe that Indians in aggregate are a truly secular and tolerant people and have demonstrated their ability to separate religion from government over a very long period of time.

DEMOCRACY

India is a heterogeneous society of people from different classes, castes, cultures, and religions. Representative democracy is government based on the voice of the people and what they want. But what do Indians want?

Indian democracy is a unique experiment in history. A mostly poor and illiterate country was given universal suffrage 66 years ago. No one really knew what the outcome of this would be. M. K. Gandhi, who is called the father of independent India, aroused the hopes and aspirations of the nation with the vision of self-reliance (called *swadeshi*) and local self-government (called *panchayiti raj*). Jawaharlal Nehru, the idealistic and socialist first prime minister of independent India, coined the term *unity in diversity* to describe the nationhood of newly independent India. He inspired the youth of the country to work with self-sacrifice for the honor of building a modern nation.

Skeptics abounded, and many believed that India would not be able to hold itself together as a nation state. In fact, the turmoil in India's neighbor and sibling, Pakistan, did not provide a good prognosis for India. It was probably India's heterogeneous character that prevented the country from throwing up a dictator and that caused it to muddle along as a democracy while Pakistan oscillated between democracy and dictatorship.

For the first 30 years after India's independence, democracy did not really work. The Indian National Congress Party under Jawaharlal Nehru won successive majorities in Parliament. While India integrated as a nation under its massive civil bureaucracy and its growing public sector or government-owned enterprises, the taste of newly acquired power in the rank-and-file of India's administrative and political classes started planting the seeds of personal greed and corruption. This was the honeymoon period of India's democracy.

After Jawaharlal Nehru's death, his daughter, Indira Gandhi, became the prime minister of India, separated by the intermittent rule of Lal Bahadur Shastri. Indira Gandhi centralized power and ruled with an iron hand. She took the country in the direction of centralized power and dictatorship. However, India was not ready for her authoritarian ways.

Democracy really started working in India only once Indira Gandhi started having political problems in the 1970s. The rise of regional leaders, first within the Indian National Congress and then with their own independent political parties, really put into motion the process of individual representation.

Post the era of Indira Gandhi, the only two times that a single party has formed a government (both times the Indian National Congress) were from 1984 to 1989, after the assassination of Indira Gandhi, and from 1991 to 1996, after the assassination of Rajiv Gandhi.

As democracy started working in India and as the people's voice started being represented, politics in India became increasingly regional and increasingly fragmented along the lines of caste, religion, and linguistic heritage. It became increasingly apparent that Nehru's idea of unity in diversity was mythical and that Indians are really a divided people.

THE RISE OF REGIONAL PARTIES

Post-independence when India was divided up into states and administrative regions, the founders of the nation decided to carve up the country along linguistic boundaries. While this strengthened federalism and created local unity of identity within the states, it created problems for the union as a whole. This also strengthened English as the medium of communication between states and for the union. Due to their common colonial legacy, states and their inhabitants were much more willing to accept English as their second language than Hindi, which was alien to many regions of the country.

Jawaharlal Nehru was accommodative of powerful state leaders within the Congress Party. However, Indira Gandhi had an autocratic reign and did not tolerate dissent in the states. She sequentially removed powerful state leaders and instated those who were loyal to her. This caused many splits within the Congress Party and also pushed powerful state leaders to form parties of their own.

Regional leaders very quickly realized that Indians were divided as a people and there was a reason why the British were so successfully able to implement *divide and rule*. Regional parties formed and succeeded on ideologies of caste, religion, economic status, language, economic ideology, and so on.

The growth of regional parties was explosive. For the first time in history, Indians in remote corners of India were able to express themselves and align with issues they truly cared about. Expression is very empowering. Empowerment is very liberating. An educated observer might remark, based on justified experiences from different parts of the world, that voting along caste or religious lines is economically detrimental and might result in outcomes that make the voter worse off. If taken to an extreme, one might espouse a modified version of the imperialistic *white man's burden*, which conveys that the illiterate masses do not know what is good for them and that someone more civilized has to benevolently uplift them. However, the reality on the ground was that Indians craved freedom and expression more than they craved economic growth, at least in the short term.

In the initial years, the expression along divided regional issues was localized and was at the village and state administration level. Regional parties also did not have the clout, vision, or financial muscle to make an impact at the national level. Policies and actions at the union level were distant and far removed from the mind space of the average Indian. However, over time, the power of the regional parties started growing, and the power of national parties started weakening.

Democracy in India has evolved and continues to mature. At first, expression was important. Now that people have been heard, they are thinking more about what they are saying and what they want.

This is where frustration for investors sets in. Different parts of India are in different stages of development. The regions of India vary based on the education and skill level of people, the economic history and industrial wealth, the work ethic and risk appetite of people, the availability of resources and infrastructure, and the aspirations of the people. However, every region has hitched its wagon to a single engine called India. The constant push and tug and cacophony of views, opinions, and desires create an explosive chaos that seems to have stalled the engine of India.

To understand where India is headed as a whole, it is important to look at the reality of the different states and regions of India.

Bihar

Bihar was once the richest region of India. The Kingdom of Magadha, to which Emperor Ashoka belonged, ruled over most of India 2,000 years ago with its seat of power in the region that is now called Bihar. The Buddha attained his enlightenment in Gaya in Bihar. Bihar also had the distinction of being the home of Asia's largest and most famous university, Nalanda University, with its origin dating back 1,500 years. Bihar is located in the great Indo-Gangetic Plains and has a fertile as well as mineral-rich landmass.

However, the history of Bihar in recent centuries has been anything but exciting. Bihar has become an overpopulated state with deep-rooted caste divisions and high rates of illiteracy. Bihar became infamous for its complete lack of industrialization and high rates of crime. The state of Jharkhand was created by carving out the forest areas of southern Bihar in 2000.

CASE STUDY: Coal India Limited

Coal India (COAL: IN) came to the limelight when the behemoth owned by the government of India went public and listed in October 2010. The company owns a large portion of India's coal reserves and accounts for 80 percent of India's coal production. It is the largest coal producer in the world and attracted substantial interest from investors when it went public. Coal India was further made infamous by the activist investor The Children's Investment Fund (TCI) of the United Kingdom. TCI acquired 1 percent of the outstanding shares of Coal India and in 2012 launched a scathing attack on the government of India, accusing it of interference in the professional management of the company and of making the company operate on nonmarket principles.

While TCI's activism against Coal India makes for an interesting soap opera and gets the fund cheap global publicity, it does very little for change in the operations of Coal India. Either the activism is a gimmick by TCI or the fund has misunderstood the company and the operations of the government of India.

Coal India is not a company; it is an entire ministry in the government of India. The Ministry of Coal of the government of India has only two significant companies under it, namely, Coal India and Neyveli Lignite Corporation. Coal India is 17 times larger than Neyveli Lignite Corporation.

Coal mining in India has had a tumultuous history centered in the states of Bihar and West Bengal. The British operated coal mines in pre-independent India under harsh conditions with almost no rights for workers. Post-independence, the entire coal mining industry moved into the hands of private operators, who operated the mines with the help of local strongmen. The plight of the workers deteriorated further under private ownership. Democratic India was in no mood to let the injustice to workers and profiteering by owners continue. In 1973, the government of India nationalized all coal mines in the country by an act of Parliament. Coal India was created in the process. The objective of nationalization was to protect the rights of workers and to bring them out of destitution as well as to bring uniformity to the regulation and operation of the country's coal mines. The company was created by the nationalization of over 900 separate coal mines, and the company continues to operate over 750 separate coal mines through seven distinct subsidiaries.

The company employs more than 350,000 workers. The government of India operated Coal India between 1975 and 2010 under 100 percent ownership on nonmarket principles with objectives other than profit maximization. The government was compelled to disinvest a portion of its holding in 2010 in order to raise resources to bridge its ever-increasing fiscal deficit. For an investor to expect that merely an initial public offering would serve as trigger and a signal for a 180-degree change in the ethos of the Ministry of Coal and the operations of Coal India would be grossly naïve. It would be dangerous for an investor to evaluate Coal India as an investment on market principles when neither the government of India nor the company has expressed any desire to change its nonmarket ways of working.

Bihar was ruled by the Congress Party for most of the time after independence until 1990. In 1990, the Congress Party was overthrown by Lalu Prasad Yadav of the Rashtriya Janata Dal. Lalu Prasad came to power with the support of the lower caste and minority vote-bank. Lalu Prasad ruled the state directly and by proxy through his wife Rabri Devi until 2005. Under Lalu Prasad, Bihar started a further backward march into poverty and did not enjoy any of the benefits of economic reforms and liberalization that were set into motion in the country in 1991.

Fascinatingly, Lalu Prasad managed to stay in power on an antidevelopment agenda. His rhetoric to the public of Bihar was that infrastructure and development only benefitted rich people and enabled them to subjugate the poor even more. Bihar had always been a source of immigrant labor for the rest of the country. However, under Lalu Prasad, the trickle turned into a flood, and young and able Biharis started leaving the state en masse to look for work elsewhere. The resentment against immigrant labor from Bihar and Uttar Pradesh that was willing to work at below-market wages and in inhospitable conditions resulted in protests and clashes in states like Assam and Maharashtra.

By the early 2000s the people of Bihar started to realize that they were being left behind while the rest of the country was marching forward. Immigrant Biharis had also seen the growth and development in other parts of the country. In 2005, Nitish Kumar of the Janata Dal United Party came to power on a development agenda.

Under Nitish Kumar, Bihar grew at double-digit growth rates consistently for five years, and Nitish Kumar was voted back to power in 2010 by the people of Bihar. Nitish Kumar rebuilt Bihar's dilapidated roads, bridges, and transport networks; he strengthened the police force and ensured the conviction of more than 39,000 criminals, who erstwhile had a free reign in Bihar. New infrastructure and housing was built in the state, and educational institutions sprang up everywhere.

However, Bihar has continued to lag behind in industrial development. Part of the reason is that infrastructure and connectivity is still inadequate and Bihar is not a large consumer market for industrial products. It is inevitable that as other parts of India grow, develop, and become more prosperous and expensive, Bihar will get its share of industrialization. Once that juggernaut sets into motion, Bihar will perhaps become one of the most sought after destinations for industrial investment in India.

Bihar's role on the national political scene has changed over the years. Once a Congress Party stronghold, under Lalu Prasad Yadav, Bihar became a wildcard. Lalu Prasad aligned with national parties wherever he got the best deal. Nitish Kumar and his Janata Dal United Party are more right leaning and were a part of the erstwhile National Democratic Alliance government that ruled the country from 1999 to 2004.

Bihar is a good example of the fragmentation taking place in India's national politics. It is very likely that as long as Nitish Kumar does a good job in Bihar, he will remain in power and get the support of the electorate. If he falters, there are numerous other regional parties ready to take his place. The ability of the two national parties, the Congress, and the Bhartiya Janata Party to make meaningful inroads into Bihar is difficult. Therefore, Bihar's representation in the national government will almost always be through a coalition.

However, the fact that Bihar has fragmented national politics does not mean that Bihar is not integrated into the Indian Union or that Bihar would want to or be better off seceding from the Union. Economically, Bihar is completely integrated into the Union as a supplier of basic materials and a buyer of manufactured products. Bihari migrants work all over India, and their remittances back home form a big part of Bihar's economy. Bihar also needs investment from companies and entrepreneurs in other prosperous parts of the country.

As has been shown in recent times, Biharis are pro-development as much as any other part of India. Investments in Bihar today are likely to be safer and more profitable than at any other time in the history of independent India. However, on the national stage, the regional party representing Bihar is likely to vote on issues in line with the needs and aspirations of Biharis at their particular stage of development. And, as discussed earlier, the needs and concerns of Biharis may not be completely aligned with the needs and concerns of people in the rest of the country.

Uttar Pradesh

Uttar Pradesh (UP) is the largest state in India. It has a population of 200 million people. The mountain state of Uttarakhand with 10 million people was carved out of UP in 2000. Bordering the capital, Delhi, UP occupies the bulk of the Indo-Gangetic Plains. UP has a representation of 80 out of 543 seats in the lower house of Parliament.

UP was ruled mostly by the Congress Party until 1989. In the ensuing period, the electorate in UP became fragmented, and the state was ruled either by a coalition of parties or in turns by the Bahujan Samaj Party (party of the backward castes), led by Mayawati, and the Samajwadi Party, led by Mulayam Singh Yadav.

At different times, UP has leaned toward socialism, religious fundamentalism, or caste-based politics. No one ever knows which way UP will vote. For a state of its size and significance, UP is a very unsettling player in national politics.

It has been proven beyond reasonable doubt that smaller states in India are better governed and administered than larger ones. The division of UP into four smaller states has been discussed many times in the past, but it has always been scuttled by vested interests.

If any place fully reflects the manifestation of India's rigid village systems, it is UP. Akhilesh Yadav, the 40-year-old son of Samajwadi Party leader Mulayam Singh Yadav, successfully ran an election campaign to defeat the incumbent Mayawati of the Bahujan Samaj Party in 2012. His youth and Western education brought hope of change to UP's rigid ways. However, it was Akhilesh Yadav who had to change. Despite a clear mandate to rule the state, Akhilesh was unable to overcome resistance to change from leaders and strongmen (who are political assets in a state like UP) within his own party.

UP is far behind Bihar in its evolution (in aggregate) and continues to be mired in religious and caste-based issues. Corruption in the state is deeply entrenched, and development is nowhere on the agenda. The fact that UP represents 80 out of 543 seats in the lower house of Parliament and is swayed by caste, religion, socialism, and populism has a telling impact on India's national politics. National and regional parties vying for influence in states like UP resort to populist measures like subsidized food, subsidized fertilizer, free power, free televisions, free bicycles, free laptops, forgiveness of farm loans, rural employment guarantee schemes, and various other giveaways that damage the fiscal health of the government, debase the currency by stealth, and crowd out much-needed private investment.

This is not a new phenomenon in India. Populism existed much before India made it into the BRICs report and much before India was *discovered* by the international investment community. The degree and intensity waxes and wanes and depends on the party in power and their desperation and insecurity. However, the good news is that populism as a way to win votes is becoming less effective. Political parties have not been able to mend their ways, but the electorate has evolved for the better.

CASE STUDY: Jaiprakash Associates

That there are companies and groups that serve as fronts for the ill-gotten wealth of powerful politicians is an open secret in India. Where the unbridled favoritism to these companies and groups ends and where quasi ownership begins is a line that is blurred and unknown. However, these groups are characterized by extreme volatility in fortunes determined by whether their benefactors are in power or not. The state of Uttar Pradesh has two such groups, the Jaypee Group that enjoys the benevolence of Mayawati of the Bahujan Samaj Party, and the Sahara group that enjoys the benevolence of Mulayam Singh of the Samajwadi Party.

Jaiprakash Associates (JPA: IN) is the flagship company of the Jaypee group. Over the years, the company has grown from being a marginal cement producer to the largest private hydropower producer, the third-largest cement producer in India, and the largest land bank owner in the National Capital Region of India (primarily in the portion that lies in the state of UP). However, the company is probably most infamous for being among the largest private-sector borrowers in the country, with a total debt of $10 billion supported by $2 billion of equity.

I have seen numerous analysts and investors, over time, try to understand the business and earnings power of Jaiprakash Associates and to try and value its stock as a potential investment. In my opinion, those analysts and investors did not have any appreciation for India's politics and the drivers behind the performance of a company like Jaiprakash Associates and of its stock. First, in my opinion, a company like Jaiprakash Associates should never find a place in the portfolio of a sensible investor due to its extremely poor standards of corporate governance and capital allocation. However, if an investor did choose to make an investment in the stock of the company, he or she would be much better served by studying the power status of Mayawati and the relationships that the owner of the company, Jaiprakash Gaur, had at any given time with the politicians in power in the Union government and in the states where the company operated its various plants than by studying the fundamentals of the company's businesses and its financial statements.

A company like Jaiprakash Associates always remains vulnerable to sudden changes in fortune both on the upside and on the downside, and its financial statements probably have no connection with the underlying reality of its various businesses.

West Bengal

West Bengal is the revolutionary state of India. It played an instrumental role in the freedom struggle against the British. The state was also the scene of numerous protest and reform movements in independent India. The violent Communist Party of India (Marxist) had its origins in West Bengal as a revolutionary movement against the *semi-feudalism* that existed in the state. The Communist Party and its various factions played a major role in the *naxalite* movement, which started in the village of Naxalbari in 1967 as a peasant uprising. The peasants demanded land reform whereby land was returned to the tiller, and the uprising was a protest against the appalling conditions of destitute landless farm labor.

In the 1960s and 1970s, the Communist Party of India (Marxist) joined India's mainstream parliamentary democracy system and it came to power in the state in 1977 on the plank of land reform. The party ruled the state continuously until 2011.

Although the capital of West Bengal, Calcutta (now renamed Kolkata), was once the capital of British India, and although it was the birthplace of most of India's large business groups, the rise of the Communist Party led to the backward march of industrial development in the state. The focus of the state shifted to land reform and agricultural development. Most large businesses relocated from Calcutta to Bombay or Delhi, and the state fell into a spiral of poverty.

CASE STUDY: Aditya Birla Group

The Birlas, along with the Tatas, are among the oldest, most well-known, and largest business groups of India. The Tata Group was headquartered in Bombay (now Mumbai) in the state of Maharashtra, and the Birla Group was headquartered in Calcutta (now Kolkata) in the state of West Bengal. Over time the Birla Group splintered into multiple subgroups the largest of which is the Aditya Birla Group, now the third-largest business conglomerate of India. The problems in the state of West Bengal and the anti-industry attitude of the Communist Party in the state forced the Aditya Birla Group to move its headquarters to Bombay (Mumbai). Not only did West Bengal lose the headquarters of the group, it saw no meaningful investments from any of the companies in the group since it chose to leave the state. The loss of West Bengal was the gain of Maharashtra and other states of India.

The largest companies of the Aditya Birla Group are Hindalco (HNDL: IN), Grasim (GRASIM: IN), Ultratech Cement (UTCEM: IN) and Idea Cellular (IDEA: IN). The group's companies have among the best standards of corporate governance and are among the best capital allocators in the country. However, the larger businesses in the group are in cyclical industries, and their fortunes cannot be separated from the state of India's macroeconomy.

However, as India started its march toward reform and economic development in the 2000s, the Communist Party under its new leader, Buddhadeb Bhattacharjee, unleashed new reforms in West Bengal. The state aspired to develop its services and manufacturing sectors and the government of West Bengal ran a massive campaign to woo private investors back to the state. However, the entire process was handled very poorly.

In its haste to demonstrate West Bengal's openness and friendliness to private capital, the government of West Bengal ran roughshod over poor landowners in the state. It assumed, erroneously, that after years of being mired in poverty, poor farmers would welcome development with open arms and would willingly part with their unprofitable land in order to get well-paying industrial and services jobs.

As discussed earlier, the controversy around the Tata Group's investment in Singur became the equivalent of the *naxalbari* episode for the Communist Party. Ironically, the up-and-coming political leader Mamata Banerjee of the Trinamool Congress Party protested the capitalistic and feudal agenda of the Communist Party and built her political career culminating with her victory in the state elections in 2011.

Mamata Banerjee and her Trinamool Congress Party are even more left leaning that the Communist Party of India. By raking up the controversy about land acquisition by force and the sentiments surrounding land, she has pushed West Bengal even farther behind in economic development. Unfortunately, the state will have to pay the price for her failed policies and only after much hardship will the people of the state come around to the development agenda. It is unlikely that West Bengal will attract meaningful investments in the foreseeable future.

West Bengal's role in national politics has always been negative. Until 2004, the Communist Party was never a meaningful player at the national level. The party became a meaningful supporter of the United Progressive Alliance (UPA) coalition government that came to power in 2004. It played a damaging role in the coalition and scuttled all attempts at reform until it was forced to leave the coalition on a stalemate over reforms related to India's civil nuclear energy policy. The Trinamool Congress became a coalition partner of the UPA-II government that came to power in 2009. However, Ms. Mamata Banerjee proved to be a worse coalition partner than the Communist Party and, after several stalemates over reforms, left the coalition in 2012.

It is unlikely that West Bengal outside of Kolkata will witness meaning-ful economic development anytime soon. The Trinamool Congress contin-ues to cause flight of private capital from the state, and the opposition led by the Communist Party has taken away the wrong reform messages from the victory of the Trinamool Congress. The population of the state is mired in the legacy of farmer oppression, and it will be a long time before they come around to the development agenda.

Irrespective of the disparity with other states of India and the large potential for catch-up, grandiose investment plans in West Bengal are likely to be challenging at best and downright suicidal at worst. West Bengal will remain a drag on India's economics as well as its politics.

Punjab and Haryana

Punjab and Haryana are the richest agricultural states of India. Inhabited by hardworking and enterprising farmers and blessed with fertile soil and plentiful water from rivers flowing down from the Himalayas, the two states are meaningful contributors to India's food production.

The people of the two states are flamboyant consumers in the Indian context and are big risk takers in their ventures. Proximity to Delhi, the national capital, has helped the states attract investments in manufacturing as well as services. The relatively affluent populations of the two states are pro-development and have enjoyed the benefits of India's economic growth.

Labor trouble in the industrial cluster of Manesar in Haryana in 2012 raised investor concern and questioned India's friendliness to foreign invest-ment. The labor trouble originated at one of Japanese carmaker Suzuki's factories located in Manesar. The trouble that started at the Suzuki fac-tory quickly spread to other factories in the cluster. However, investigations revealed that the trouble was specific to Suzuki's poor handling of labor relations and was exaggerated by the subsequent involvement of political elements that tried to benefit from the trouble. It was by no means representative of a larger systemic problem in either the population or the administration of the state of Haryana.

It is likely that Punjab and Haryana will be active participants and contributors to India's economic growth. They are also very open to investment and development of India's farm sector and retail industry. The largest investments and biggest innovations in the areas of corporate farming and organized retail are likely to emerge from these two states.

Punjab and Haryana have played a stabilizing role in India's national politics and have generally been invisible contributors to India's parliamentary democracy.

CASE STUDY: Contract Farming and the Second Green Revolution

Agriculture in post-independence India was in a dismal state. Floods, droughts, and famines were common occurrences, and farmers lived in destitution. India's agricultural research institutes, in collaboration with American scientists and universities, ushered in a green revolution in India in the 1960s and 1970s. High-yielding varieties of grain were introduced together with the increased usage of chemical fertilizers and pesticides. Irrigation systems were improved, and credit was made available to farmers. Agricultural output and productivity increased dramatically, and India became self-sufficient in food.

As India continues to grow and the upward mobility of its population increases, with the demand for more and better-quality food, India is in need of a second green revolution. To usher in a second green revolution, India needs to improve its agricultural supply chain, and it needs to reduce wastage in the system. The country needs to embrace contract farming that provides farmers economies of scale in focused varieties of produce and derisks them from the vagaries of selling their produce. Punjab and Haryana are the most agriculturally progressive states and are at the forefront of this revolution.

Companies like McDonald's and Pepsico have been entering into long-term purchase contracts with farmers who agree to grow certain varieties of produce (potatoes, tomatoes, etc.) to fulfill the captive needs of their outlets in India. Companies like Reliance Retail and Field Fresh from Bharti Enterprises have been entering into purchase contracts with farmers to sell produce through their wholesale and retail stores as well to export produce. Companies like ITC, Hindustan Unilever, and Kellogg have been using contract farming to feed their food-processing plants with high-quality, standardized produce at stable contracted prices.

While farmers in Punjab and Haryana have been at the forefront of this change, the real impact on India's agricultural productivity and farm income levels will be felt when farmers in other states start following in their footsteps.

Gujarat and Rajasthan

Gujarat and Rajasthan are the entrepreneur states of India. Large parts of both states are barren deserts, and consequently the populations of these parts of the states have always relied on trading and business as their source of livelihood. They have also been willing migrants in search of entrepreneurial opportunities.

While Rajasthanis (a subset of whom are called Marwaris) traditionally migrated to other parts of India in search of opportunities, Gujaratis migrated to all parts of the world and comprise a significant part of India's global Diaspora.

The state of Rajasthan itself remained quite economically backward for most of the period post independence. However, Gujarat was at the forefront of industrial development, with its large coastline attracting large-scale investments in process-oriented industries like industrial chemicals, refineries, petrochemicals, textiles, and pharmaceuticals.

Gujarat has benefitted from its enterprising population as well as from stable political leadership over the decades. Home to a large Muslim population (albeit minority) and an activist Hindu population, Gujarat has also been a hotbed of religious and communal tension.

The state has been ruled since 1990 by non-Congress governments and has been a stronghold of the Bharatiya Janata Party since 1995. Narendra Modi of the Bharatiya Janata Party, who came to power in 2001, has been the only leader to win a third consecutive term as chief minister of Gujarat.

Gujarat has been the darling of private capital and has been one of the most pro-capitalist states of India since independence. It has welcomed immigrant labor and has created capacity for growth in terms of physical infrastructure and institutional infrastructure as well as human capital.

It is likely that Gujarat will continue to attract private investment and grow at high rates independent of the state of affairs of the Indian Union. If things at the Union level were to fix themselves, Gujarat would be a disproportionate beneficiary and would witness an economic boom of unprecedented proportions.

Maharashtra

Maharashtra was the biggest beneficiary of the troubles that plagued Calcutta and West Bengal in the period after independence. It was the first industrial state of India. Entrepreneurs from all parts of India moved to Maharashtra's capital, Bombay, and it became the commercial capital of the country. Bombay built a very large textile industry in the 1950s and 1960s and is the home of the financial markets of the country.

However, a crippling textile strike in 1982 destroyed the industry in Bombay and resulted in a mass exodus of textile enterprises from the city. Bombay has also been a hotbed of religious and communal tension in the country and has been witness to massive religious riots as well as several terrorist attacks.

Maharashtra is a large state outside of Bombay (now renamed Mumbai). It is physically the third-largest state of India and with 112 million people has the second-largest population in the country. Maharashtra has a very large agricultural as well as industrial base. Mumbai is the crown jewel of Maharashtra, and the state significantly benefits from the revenues that Mumbai generates. Mumbai suffers for being a part of Maharashtra since its electorate is unable to influence who rules the state due to its small size but has to carry a disproportionate burden of funding the state.

It has often been commented that Mumbai would be significantly better off if it were carved out as a separate state from Maharashtra similar to Delhi. Given how much Maharashtra needs Mumbai and given that Maharashtra's legislature has to vote in favor of the move, a split like that is never likely to happen. Mumbai's fate therefore will remain tied to the fortunes of Maharashtra.

Since the 1990s, Maharashtra has experienced significant political instability and an endemic rise in corruption. From being the first choice for private investments, the state has fallen to third place behind Gujarat and Tamil Nadu. The state has a very well developed industrial base with excellent physical and institutional infrastructure, world-class enterprises, and well-developed human capital. This base is being eroded by an absence of leadership and by political mismanagement. Maharashtra has also played a fragmenting role in national politics.

In many ways, the story of Maharashtra is the story of India. It is a state with tremendous potential that is suffering due to the absence of effective leadership and governance.

Odisha, Jharkhand, and Chattisgarh

The three eastern states of Odisha, Jharkhand, and Chattisgarh are in the forest belt of India. They are also among the most mineral-rich states of the country. Traditionally inhabited by large tribal communities, large parts of the states are inaccessible and have poor to nonexistent infrastructure and connectivity.

These states are among the poorest and most underdeveloped in India and have a combined population of almost 100 million people. Large parts of these states are under no formal administration, and the government of India has virtually no control over the activities in these regions. The lack of development and destitution of the population has led to the development of left-wing guerilla armies collectively branded as *Maoists*. Mineral-rich areas are also under the control of local mafias.

Despite their mineral wealth and untapped pool of workers, these states have not been able to benefit from or contribute to India's growth and development. It seems that democracy has played a detrimental role (from a conventional viewpoint) in the economic development of these states. Several large showcase investment projects in these states have been scuttled due to environmental indecision on the part of the state and the union government as well as local protests.

CASE STUDY: The Vedanta Group and the Niyamgiri Hills

Indian billionaire Anil Agarwal, who owned Vedanta Aluminum (VED: LN), set up a 1 million tonne per year aluminum smelter in Lanjigarh, Odisha, at a cost of $1 billion. The refinery employed 5,500 people and had a mining license for bauxite from the nearby Niyamgiri hills. The government of India revoked both forest and mining licenses for the project, and it became embroiled in a controversy surrounding local tribes.

The irony of the situation is that Vedanta had obtained a mining permit from the Union government as well as the state government before proceeding with its investment in the aluminum smelter. However, the opposition by local tribes was picked up by certain nongovernmental organizations (NGOs) and special-interest groups. Very quickly, the media and politicians got involved in the mix. Vedanta was singled out as the evil RDA from James Cameron's film *Avatar* trying to mine unobtanium (bauxite) from the sacred Hometree (Niyamgiri hills) that the Na'avi (Dongria Kondh) tribe had prayed to for centuries.

The controversy reached the Supreme Court of India, and it ruled that local tribes who considered the hill sacred should decide the fate of the mining license based on a local vote. Twelve villages with a total population of 900 people voted against mining in the Niyamgiri hills, and a billion dollars of investment as well as 5,500 direct jobs and thousands of indirect jobs were jeopardized.

In the absence of a clear law and rules that deal with the trade-off between economic development, the environment, and society, and in the absence of a government with leadership that has the will to enforce the law and rules, India's natural resource sector has failed to live up to its potential and has remained hostage to media trials and minority opinion like the one that derailed Vedanta's investment in the mineral-rich state of Odisha.

India has been unable to make up its mind on the balance it seeks to achieve between development, environment, and society. It is impossible to leave the environment untouched if the country seeks development and an improvement in standards of living for hundreds of millions of people. It is possible to put in place strict, transparent, and unambiguous rules that safeguard the environment and minimize the impact of development. The same holds true for impact on society through displacement caused by large development projects that invariably require land previously under alternate use.

India is in an evolving phase with respect to this debate. That a consensus is being sought and ambiguous and conflicting rules and laws are being tested and challenged is healthy for the country and for investments in the country. The process is painful to endure, unpleasant to watch, and expensive in terms of financial losses and opportunity costs. Given India's deep-rooted democratic ethos, there is no other way to go about it. The hope is that once India makes up its mind, the momentum that will build will be strong, irreversible, and with the support of all stakeholders making it more sustainable and permanent. Until that happens, India will continue to showcase itself in a poor light and will possibly miss out on several potential short-term and significant opportunities.

Andhra Pradesh

Andhra Pradesh was traditionally a Congress Party stronghold. In 1983, the movie actor turned politician N. T. Rama Rao's Telugu Desam Party overthrew the Congress and came to power with a clear mandate. N. T. Rama Rao was a populist leader, and under his rule the state continued to remain mired in poverty.

The Telugu Desam Party was briefly displaced by the Congress Party from 1989 to 1994. In 1994, the Telugu Desam Party under N. T. Rama Rao came back to power in the state. N. T. Rama Rao fell ill in 1995 and passed away in 1996. N. T. Rama Rao's son-in-law, Chandrababu Naidu, took his place as chief minister.

Chandrababu Naidu unleashed a transformation of Andhra Pradesh that took it from one of the worst-performing states of India to one of its best performing. He cleaned up the state capital, Hyderabad; built infrastructure; and attracted the information technology (IT) industry to Andhra Pradesh. He was reelected for a second term in 1999. Under his leadership, the IT industry in Andhra Pradesh became the second largest in India.

Chandrababu Naidu famously laid out a 20-year vision and plan for the transformation of Andhra Pradesh. His reign was unfortunately cut short, and in one of the biggest election surprises of the time, the Congress Party under Y. S. Rajasekhara Reddy came to power in 2004 with a clear majority. The unexpected defeat of Chandrababu Naidu in the Andhra Pradesh state elections coincided with the unexpected defeat of the Bharatiya Janata Party–led National Democratic Alliance in the national general elections.

What emerged with this episode was that even though urban India had done well and had benefitted from reforms and progressive liberalization, rural India was under stress and in a very unhappy place. For the rural population, India was anything but *shining*. It is often commented that Chandrababu was not given sufficient time by the electorate to fully implement his vision for the state. Had he stayed on, he would've transformed Andhra Pradesh at both the urban and the rural levels.

Y. S. R. Reddy ruled the state with an iron hand and was a very strong and successful administrator. He had several strong-arm tactics up his sleeve, and he permitted and quashed political protest movements as per his political convenience.

Y. S. R. Reddy was given a clear mandate for a second term in 2009. Unfortunately, he died in a helicopter crash in 2009, plunging the state into political chaos. During the period from 2009 to 2014, the state was effectively ruled by the Congress Party high command in Delhi. They had no clue of the ground reality, and the state declined into economic chaos.

Andhra Pradesh is a very agriculturally rich state. It has also witnessed significant industrial development along it ports and in Hyderabad. Despite that, large parts of the state are poorly accessible and influenced by the guerilla *maoist* insurgency.

Andhra Pradesh has tremendous potential for growth and development. The population of the state is very development oriented and enterprising. While a big percentage of the state's population is engaged in farming and continues to be influenced by populist policies in that realm, the population of the state is, in general, pro-business.

Tamil Nadu

If there is any state in India that exhibits secessionist tendencies, it is the southern Indian state of Tamil Nadu, the state where I live.

The reorganization of India into states based on linguistic boundaries created problems in states like Tamil Nadu. The population of the state strongly opposed the imposition of Hindi as the *national language* in the state. Protest movements against the imposition of language and against the perceived subjugation of the ethnically different *Dravidian* population of the state in the 1960s led to a shift of power from the Congress Party to the regional party, the Dravida Munnetra Kazhagam (DMK). Since the DMK came to power in 1967, the state has never voted for a national party. The state has been ruled alternately by DMK and by its breakaway faction the All India Anna Dravida Munnetra Kazhagam (AIADMK) since 1967.

The capital of Tamil Nadu is Chennai (earlier known as Madras). Chennai is India's fourth-largest city by population and one of its most economically and industrially developed cities. It is located on the southeast coast of India, with one of the country's busiest ports. The state is highly literate and very economically advanced. It competes with Gujarat for the mantle of the fastest-growing state in India.

Tamil Nadu has by far the best human capital in India and it has a very hardworking and industrious population. The state has a very large indigenous entrepreneur community and the state is pro-business. Under the rule of the DMK and the AIADMK, corruption has become deeply entrenched in the state.

Tamil Nadu, other than a brief period in the 1960s, did not go in the direction of secessionism, and demands have been more in the direction of autonomy and protection of the federal structure that is guaranteed by the constitution of India. The economy of the state is very deeply entrenched in the national supply chain of goods and services, and Tamil Nadu is a strategic base for many large enterprises servicing the national market. Over the years, the state has opened up and integrated with the rest of the country. The state today is more progressive and pro-development than it has ever been in the past. The state has attracted a lot of foreign investment in manufacturing and is one of the preferred destinations for Korean, Japanese, and French companies investing in India.

The state plays a very divisive role in national politics. The DMK and the AIADMK are known to extract their meaningful pound of flesh in exchange for their support to national coalition governments. National coalitions can never be certain of their support, and their agenda remains solely focused on the development of Tamil Nadu, which may or may not be completely in sync with the national agenda at all times. It is unlikely that the Congress Party or the Bharatiya Janata Party will win meaningful votes in the state, and it is most likely that Tamil Nadu will remain a coalition player and contributor at the national level, at least for the foreseeable future.

Delhi

Delhi is the capital of India and is a quasi-state governed by a legislative assembly and a chief minister. Until 1993, the state was under direct rule of the president of India as a territory of the India Union. It achieved partial statehood with a legislative assembly in 1993, almost at the same time as the start of India's economic liberalization in 1991. Delhi, together with bordering regions from the states of Haryana and Uttar Pradesh, is commonly referred to as the National Capital Region (NCR).

Delhi was ruled by the Bharatiya Janata Party from 1993 to 1998 and was ruled by Sheila Dikshit of the Congress Party continuously from 1998 to 2013. The period of independent statehood for Delhi has been transformative. The infrastructure of Delhi went from being nonexistent to world class in a short span of 20 years. Delhi has recorded among the highest rates of growth and investment in the country and remains pro-business and development.

Delhi is the only completely urban state in India with a meaningful population of 12 million people. It is the only state in India that votes based on middle-class issues and concerns and is not swayed by agricultural and rural considerations. The outcome is telling. The government of Sheila Dikshit managed to win three consecutive terms to office by giving the citizens of Delhi more effective administration and higher-quality infrastructure and standard of living than prior ones. The gap between Delhi and other cities of India is stark, and this gap is likely to continue to widen over time due to Delhi's independent statehood and administration.

The economic growth of Delhi was accompanied by a rapid influx of population that led to a deterioration in the quality of public goods and services. The growth was also accompanied by a rapid increase in corruption and crime. The middle-class population of Delhi revolted against the fifteen year rule of the Congress Party and elected the minority government of Arvind Kejriwal of the Aam Aadmi Party (AAP)—literally, the common man's party—in December 2013. AAP has taken away the wrong message from its election victory and has veered towards urban populism. How the politics and development of Delhi will unfold remains to be seen.

COMPETITION AMONG STATES IS HEALTHY

Since the start of India's economic liberalization in 1991, India has attracted a lot of foreign investment and a lot of foreign interest in potential investment. Several states, such as Gujarat, Tamil Nadu, and Andhra Pradesh, were early off the mark in competing for these investments. Other states, such as Odisha and West Bengal, made feeble attempts at attracting investments; however, the follow-through in these states was poor.

The competition among states for investment is very healthy for India and for potential investors. It keeps extreme ideology in check and makes the people of the various states realize that investment capital (foreign and domestic) is a privilege and cannot be taken for granted.

India, as envisioned by its constitution is a federation of states, and significant powers vest with state governments. National policies and a lack of them can inhibit or encourage growth and investment; however, a lot can still be done by individual state governments within their legislative powers even in the absence of progress or support at the level of the Union. This is clearly borne out by the different rates of growth of states within the country.

As regional parties become more powerful and as national governments become formed by larger coalitions, federalism in India is strengthening, and the power of states is increasing. In the case of controversial policy reforms like foreign investment in organized retail, after much heartburn, the Union government has resorted to setting out the overall big-picture policy framework but has left the actual speed, size, and implementation of the framework to individual state governments. States like Punjab and Haryana, whose farmers are likely to be big beneficiaries of organized retail, are likely to embrace foreign investment in large-format, organized retail much more willingly and quickly than states like West Bengal, where the left-leaning leadership remains afraid of the unknown and remains unwilling to rock the boat with respect to the livelihood of mom-and-pop retail. One can rationally extrapolate that once the benefits of a particular change become visible in one state, the ability of other states to resist it will diminish significantly.

For investors looking at India, this is one of the biggest opportunities and one of the biggest challenges. Given the state of India's politics, the approach to India will have to be on a state-by-state and region-by-region basis. A blind pan-India strategy based on policies of the Union government alone will result in expensive mistakes and disappointments. While in an ideal world it would be great to have uniformity of thought and purpose and to have a single India strategy, given the size of India and the size of individual states, it will be prudent for investors to build a regional strategy as well as a national strategy.

THE GOODS AND SERVICES TAX

While India is a federation in matters of policy, legislation, and jurisdiction, it is also not a single common market for goods and services. Basic economies of scale that can be achieved by sourcing raw materials from some states, producing goods and services in others states, and selling products in several others cannot be achieved in India due to a labyrinthine and archaic system of cascading and burdensome indirect taxes.

Policy makers both at the Union and state levels have been working seriously to arrive at a consensus on the implementation of the goods and services tax (GST), which will eliminate the cascading impact of taxes and make India into a single common market. The benefits of this tax reform will be significantly large and will provide a big boost for investment activity in the Indian economy.

Even as India is moving in the direction of increased federalism and increased devolution of policy-making powers to the states, the GST will involve some sacrifice of sovereignty and control over tax revenue generation ability of the states. States have been worried, and legitimately so, that giving up too much power over the ability to generate revenue might jeopardize their ability to direct policy making for their individual states.

The UPA-II administration, in its election manifesto of 2009, had promised the implementation of the GST by April 1, 2010. The policy has eluded the administration, and the consensus building has been a very public and frustrating affair for businesspeople, investors, and policy makers alike. In India's democratic setup, this is the only way to go about doing it. Expediency notwithstanding, if one were to take a step back and take a long-term developmental view, it is only appropriate that mega policy reforms like the GST should be implemented after addressing the concerns of all stakeholders, after building consensus, and after getting the buy-in of all constituents. India clearly has a track record of taking consensus building and due process too far; however, treading a middle path is probably appropriate. The good news here is that significant headway has been made on the GST, and it is likely that it will be implemented sooner rather than later. For businesses and investors, the good news will be that when GST is implemented, it will be a progressive and permanent change for India with no risk of reversal.

IS DEMOCRACY HOLDING INDIA BACK?

Democracy has played a role in unifying India in ways that the founders of independent India could not have imagined. When the British left India, it was a motley mix of provinces, princely states, and protectorates. The only thing that held India together in the colonial period was the force and fear of an external occupier. Once the British left India, it might very well have disintegrated into a number of small warring states and principalities. What unified India was Gandhi's vision of local self-government and devolution of power to the people under a federal structure.

The rise of regional parties and state-level upheavals show that democracy in India works. Representative democracy in India has succeeded beyond anyone's imagination. Nobody knows which way India will vote because elections are the verdict of the people, and in India the needs and aspirations of a large and young population are changing dramatically and at a very rapid pace.

Democracy does slow down the decision-making process in India. There are many decisions that can perhaps never be made in India that can be made in other parts of the world. In India it is very difficult to displace a large number of people in the name of development and growth. Mumbai International Airport has struggled to get rid of slums that illegally occupy land that belongs to it and that it needs desperately to expand runways and airport facilities for the growth of Mumbai and India. These slums form a part of Dharavi, the largest slum in Asia, which has a population of more than 1 million people and constitutes a significant voter base. Even though all the people there are poor and illegal encroachers, in numbers they equal the voters in the wealthy areas of South Mumbai.

One often hears the question that, with so much talent and potential, why can't India be more like Singapore or China? The answer probably is that because that is perhaps not what Indians want first and foremost. Perhaps what they want first and foremost is freedom and empowerment. They want to deal with their petty and mundane issues first, and they want their voice to be heard. One could argue that they don't know what is good for them and some benevolent individual or party should make the appropriate choices for them. It would be very hard to fathom how one individual or party could decide what is good for 1.2 billion people, especially because their needs and wants are most likely to be conflicting.

People know what is good for them. They know what they want no matter how poor or illiterate. Someone approaching the situation from a different context might argue that what they want is not good for them, but that is just a point of view and can lead to philosophical debate about absolute and relative outcomes and the meaning of good and bad. Democracy works. It makes the system self-correcting. It provides the system with a pressure release valve that manifests itself on a daily basis and reduces the risk of a spectacular collapse. Because outcomes in a democracy are the result of the collective action of millions of participants, the system develops automatic stabilizers. When one looks at the fall of dictatorial regimes around the world, one wonders what caused them to collapse. One wonders what led to an unraveling of the social order of the Soviet Union, Egypt, and Iraq. Could the same thing happen in China or Singapore? These are meaningful questions to ask when making long-term investments in a market.

India presents a very large opportunity. It is perhaps the largest real opportunity that has emerged in the world in a very long time. However, the economy is likely to follow its own developmental model and path and will require strategies and solutions that are unique to it. Looking at another market or economy and wondering why the same thing cannot or does not happen in India, or looking at India and wondering why certain things happen, only leads to frustration and confusion.

Democracy by itself does not absolve India of all its problems and the need for action. There are a very large number of things that are wrong with India that need to be fixed. If India does not take decisive and relatively quick actions, it is likely that its economy will suffer in a big way. India needs to accelerate the process of consensus building and needs bold and effective leadership to make difficult choices that inevitably need to be made on the path to development and growth.

Indians need to think much harder about things like why a city like Delhi succeeds (relatively speaking) but a city like Mumbai fails miserably. Does it make sense to carve out Mumbai as a state separate from the state of Maharashtra? How do entire states like Gujarat or Tamil Nadu succeed while entire states like Odisha fail? The good news is that by trial and error and through the process of self-correction, India and Indians are maturing rapidly. They realize that growth and development is the only way for them to achieve their aspirations. Some slower and some faster, but gradually all Indians will come around to the consensus on development that will lead to the explosive growth of India. When will it happen? Nobody knows, but I believe that we are far ahead on that path and the tipping point is close.

STATE OF POLITICAL AFFAIRS IN INDIA

The Congress Party came to power in 1991, forming a minority government with the outside support of coalition partners. The assassination of Congress President Rajiv Gandhi during the elections created a wave similar to the one that had brought Rajiv Gandhi to power in 1984 after the assassination of his mother, Indira Gandhi. P. V. Narasimha Rao became the prime minister, and Manmohan Singh became the finance minister of India.

Economically, India was in a terrible state when Narasimha Rao took over the reins of the country. The Gulf War had resulted in a skyrocketing of oil prices that had debilitated India's balance of payments. The period between 1989 and 1991 also saw the emergence of the third front, and India saw two prime ministers in two years. The two years were a very chaotic period for India, and the country saw widespread protest movements and agitations for and against various government policies.

In this backdrop, India ran out of foreign exchange in May 1991. None of its creditors were willing to lend to India, and the country had to airlift its gold reserves to the Bank of England to secure an emergency line of credit. India had hit its nadir, and the country was humiliated. In his budget of July 1991, Manmohan Singh unleashed economic reforms and kick-started what has since been referred to as India's economic liberalization.

While Manmohan Singh has been called the architect of India's economic liberalization, in my opinion he has been given undue credit. Economic liberalization of India had been discussed for a long time, and in 1991 it was an idea whose time had come. Manmohan Singh really did not have too many other options. If anyone should get the credit for liberalization, it should be P. V. Narasimha Rao because it was his leadership and steadfastness that enabled Manmohan Singh to do what he did.

As India weathered an economic crisis, it was also enduring a social crisis that had been simmering under the hood since independence. This was the communal tension between the Hindu majority population of India and the Muslim minority population. By maintaining separate civil codes and by providing different rules and protections to the two communities, the founding fathers of independent India institutionalized the communal divide between the Hindus and Muslims that had existed for centuries. The flame of the divide had further been fanned by minority appeasement and vote bank politics by almost all political parties. By the time the government of Narasimha Rao took office, the country was in a frenzy of communal tension. Right wing fundamentalist Hindu groups demolished the Babri Masjid in December 1992. The Babri Masjid was a mosque that had allegedly been built on the birthplace of a Hindu god by Muslim invaders centuries ago.

The demolition of the mosque was followed by widespread communal riots all over India, but especially in Bombay (now Mumbai). The aftermath of the riots saw a series of powerful bomb blasts in Bombay in 1993 masterminded by exiled mob bosses and their local henchmen (almost all Muslim).

By 1996, the euphoria that had followed the liberalization of the country had also started to fizzle out, and the stark reality of the task that lay ahead was dawning upon people. The Congress Party was not able to win a reelection in 1996, and India once again ended up with a third front coalition government. The outcome was terrible. India had three prime ministers in a two-year period. The world was experiencing the Asian crisis, soon to be followed by the Russian and Long-Term Capital Management crisis. In such an environment, Atal Bihari Vajpayee of the Bharatiya Janata Party emerged as the leader of choice, and the Bharatiya Janata Party formed the government in March 1998. In May 1998, India conducted a series of nuclear tests that resulted in the imposition of sanctions against the country and further exacerbated the economic slowdown in the country.

Vajpayee's government could last for only 13 months and the country had to endure general elections again in 1999. In May 1999, Atal Bihari Vajpayee once again became the prime minister of India as the leader of the National Democratic Alliance coalition, of which the Bharatiya Janata Party was the largest constituent. This time, he managed to serve his full term of five years.

Vajpayee's government unleashed a slew of reforms and put the country on the path of reform that helped it achieve several years of high-single-digit growth rates. In 2003, the National Democratic Alliance (NDA) launched the *India Shining* campaign that showcased the achievements of its government as well as to highlight the promising future of India. However, just like Chandrababu Naidu in Andhra Pradesh had failed to recognize the simmering rural discontent, the NDA got carried away by the success it had achieved with the urban middle class. In one of the biggest election upsets in history, the NDA lost the general election, and Chandra Babu Naidu's Telugu Desam Party lost the state elections in Andhra Pradesh to the Congress Party.

To counter the NDA's India Shining campaign, the United Progressive Alliance, the coalition government led by the Congress Party, launched the campaign for *inclusive growth*. As urban India was getting rich, rural India was in a state of crisis. Two successive droughts in 2001 and 2002 had destroyed rural livelihoods, and voters in the hinterland were angry. The UPA government launched the biggest populist transfer in the history of India, and, in the garb of inclusive growth, completely destroyed India's fiscal balance sheet.

They artificially capped fuel and fertilizer prices that were starting to become market price linked in the NDA regime. They started a massive food procurement program with continuously rising farm support prices. They launched a rural employment guarantee scheme and a giant farm loan forgiveness program.

From being right leaning during the NDA regime, India had gone full circle to being socialist and left leaning during the UPA regime. The even bigger surprise was the reelection of the UPA government in 2009, and with a stronger mandate than in 2004. The UPA-II administration took the wrong message of invincibility away from this and let loose an unprecedented wave of corruption and cronyism. It was time for the urban middle classes to revolt, and large anticorruption protests gripped the entire country. With a complete vacuum of leadership at the top, bickering broke out among the various ministries and their territorial ministers and bureaucrats, and India plunged into a state of policy paralysis.

BUREAUCRACY

The British administered India through the Imperial Civil Service. After India became independent, the home minister of India, Sardhar Vallabhbhai Patel, encouraged the formation of the Indian Civil Services based on impartiality and merit. The Indian Administrative Service (IAS) formed the backbone of India's administrative machinery. The IAS created an educated and meritocratic class of elite administrators who hailed from the length and breadth of the country. Beyond providing continuity and quality of governance, the civil services played an invaluable role in uniting the country.

However, over time, left unchecked, India's bureaucracy started to get corrupted and territorial. Every Union ministry has a minister and deputy minister and/or ministers of state also called *netas* and a secretary and several joint secretaries and additional secretaries also called *babus*. The babus run the country, supposedly under the direction of the netas. However, given the short shelf life of most netas in India, they always operate from a position of incomplete knowledge and information. The babus are aware of this and play this to their full advantage. There is constant bickering between bureaucrats in different ministries and all kinds of vested interests at play all the time. In the absence of strong leadership at the top, bureaucrats have the ability to bring decision making in the country to a grinding halt.

Recent corruption scandals in India have resulted in backlash and witch-hunt against both politicians and bureaucrats, and the effect has been a seizing up of all decision making and action. Indian bureaucrats are a classic case of a good system having run amok in the absence of strong leadership and vision in the country for an extended period.

CORRUPTION AND RENT SEEKING

Corruption is a subject that evokes very strong sentiments in people. It evokes a sense of rage among Indians and a sense of exasperation among foreigners who deal with India. India is rife with corruption, as are many other parts of the world. The issue of corruption in India is blown out of proportion. I don't endorse or condone corruption and agree that not having it is much better than having it. However, observers get caught up in the emotion of corruption and draw all kinds of wrong conclusions.

Corruption is inevitable. Corruption is no different from the real estate market. It is based on the concept of rent seeking. The owner, controller, or gatekeeper of a resource seeks to extract the maximum rent possible from the potential user of the resource within the context of alternatives available to the user.

When one sees an increase in rates of corruption, it is usually accompanied by underlying growth and an increase in the quantum of spoils available to go around. It is similar to an increase in rents in a city with low vacancy rates and booming business. In that context, the market for corruption is self-correcting. In India today, every businessperson worth his salt is complaining about corruption. This is because the growth and the corresponding spoils have disappeared, but the rents of corruption have not come down. None of these people were complaining when the times were good because they were busy jockeying for influence and driving rents higher. Their disgust with corruption at this time is part of the price-correction mechanism of corruption to align with a tempered economic outlook. One would be naïve to assume that there is a major cleansing process under way and that corruption is likely to reduce or go away in India.

Let us, then, look at how an individual or a group of individuals become controllers or gatekeepers of valuable resources. Here, the good news is that India's efficiently functioning democracy has created a relatively free market in the control of resources. If one were to consider oneself an entrepreneur and objectively explore the prospects of entering into the business of control of resources and rent seeking (corruption), one would realize that the business is really not as lucrative as one would think. India's democracy ensures that the business of corruption has not created wealthy individuals like Vladimir Putin and Muamar Gaddafi that authoritarian regimes have created.

The ultimate seed of corruption in a democracy like India, as in other democracies, lies in the problem of campaign finance. It is expensive to contest elections and is getting more so. If one were to believe that individuals and corporations would finance political campaigns without getting their ends served, one would be delusional. In efficiently functioning democracies like India, rents extracted by people and parties while in power are almost always spent away in the quest for staying in office and in getting reelected to office.

Indian administrators and politicians have taken the market for control of resources to a whole new level. The entire administrative machinery in India has institutionalized corruption. Every single position of power and influence in the government, from a sales tax inspector of a commercially busy region all the way up to the minister of a ministry with substantial resources and power, has a price. The price of this position is based on the quantum of corruption rent that the position can economically earn over the duration of its term and is paid up the chain in fractions leading all the way up to the top. The top then becomes a collection agency for these fractional amounts that can become meaningful sums when aggregated. The top then inevitably ends up spending all resources back into the system to keep the particular administration in office.

There is a very interesting anecdote of an election campaign speech by Bansi Lal, a former chief minister of the state of Haryana, who exhorted the public to reelect him to office. Being a brash *jat* (a stereotype similar to the one attributed to Texans) from Haryana, he openly appealed to the public that they were better off voting for him because he had been in office for a while and his stomach was full (with the fruits of corruption), whereas any new person they would elect was likely to fleece them a lot more because they were likely to be poor and hungry. Fortunately, the public of Haryana did not heed his advice, and he lost the election.

One of the consequences of an institutionally corrupt system is that a modified form of Gresham's Law comes into play, and corrupt individuals drive out noncorrupt individuals until the entire system becomes flooded with corrupt individuals. It becomes very risky for a corrupt system to have noncorrupt actors inhabiting it, and the entire system goes after the noncorrupt individual, forcing him or her to either become complicit or to leave.

When one looks at corruption, one has to evaluate the role of the giver almost as much as one evaluates the role of the receiver of bribes. One then realizes that most people are fairly comfortable with the idea of paying bribes. They obviously justify and rationalize it away either as a *bakshish* (tip) for efficient service or as *speed money* for efficiently achieving their economic interests. The giver and the receiver are the yin and yang of corruption that cannot be separated.

In the case of petty corruption, people often rationalize away demands for bribes with the theory that since the government does not pay officials enough to sustain a reasonable standard of living, they have no choice but to turn to bribes to augment their standard of living. In this case, people are not troubled by the existence of corruption because their bribes are unlikely to help the receiving officials live lives that are significantly better than those of average people. However, it is very large-scale corruption, where the beneficiaries live extravagant lives at the expense of ordinary citizens, that enrages people. The rage is to a large extent driven by a sense of an absence of fairness and equity.

What impact does corruption have on the Indian economy and its prospects? It does have an impact, but not in the context that popular opinion would have one believe. Corruption sometimes results in misdirection and misallocation of resources to where the highest rents can be derived and not necessarily where the resources can be used most productively. Corruption often also results in inferior quality of outcomes driven by classic game theory where everyone is worse off.

Corruption will not go away in India. As long as there are positions of power and independence of decision making, it will stay. Everyone (the giver and the receiver) is in it for something and therein lies the root cause of the corruption. There is no benevolence in the process. It might be a cynical view, but it is the truth. Corruption is not a problem as long as the pie is growing larger and as long as the system is self-correcting and has automatic checks and balances in place.

When there is enough to go around and people don't have to jostle for their piece of the cake, an evolved electorate will probably vote for a decline in corruption. Until then, if you seek to invest in India, be prepared to see the footprints of corruption all around you.

WAR, TERRORISM, AND VIOLENCE

Indians are a very nonviolent people. I am not sure whether Indians became nonviolent because of Gandhi or whether Gandhi was able to preach nonviolence because of its inherent acceptance in Indian society. My hunch is that it is the latter. While some inhabitants of certain regions of India are relatively more assertive and violent than those of other regions, in the global context, Indians in aggregate are quite nonviolent. The reason can be probably attributed to the fact that the dominant religions with their origin in India—Buddhism, Jainism, and Hinduism—are tolerant and prescribe nonviolence.

However, parts of India have leaned in the direction of armed rebellion due to large-scale mismanagement by the government. The northeast of India has seen an increase in armed guerilla groups due to insensitivity on the part of the government of India on the real issues in the region and its inability to address them. The state of Jammu and Kashmir in the north has been mismanaged by successive governments, starting with the first government of independent India under Jawaharlal Nehru. It remains an unresolved problem and continues to remain a flashpoint between India and Pakistan. The tribal areas in the eastern forest belt of India have seen armed rebellion by left-wing *Maoist* groups. This is due to a complete failure of administration in these regions by the government of India.

While these areas remain unstable for private investment and remain a drag on India's resources and its potential, their ability to derail activity in other parts of India remains low. The bigger challenge and the disturbing trend in recent times has been that of local minority support for externally funded terrorist activities due to disillusionment toward (alleged) unequal treatment by the government and by the dominant majority in the private sector. There is no easy fix for this problem, and just like in the rest of the world, terrorism is here to stay.

Geopolitically, India finds itself in a very unfavorable place. The government's foreign strategy and exercise of economic diplomacy is extremely disappointing. Successive governments have been so distracted by affairs at home that they have not been able to build on and execute a consistent and directed foreign policy. While on the one hand India is surrounded by neighbors that are almost all failing states—Pakistan, Nepal, Bangladesh, and Sri Lanka—on the other hand, it has a behemoth neighbor in China to the north with a visionary and aggressive geopolitical strategy. China's aggressive build out of infrastructure in completely inhospitable regions like Tibet has raised alarm bells in India, and rightly so. Despite this, I don't believe that South Asia remains a flashpoint, and I do not believe that India will be a part of a major war in the region anytime soon.

ROLE OF THE FOURTH ESTATE AND ACCOUNTABILITY

Freedom of the press is guaranteed by the constitution of India. India truly has a vibrant and free press. Or does it? While the press is free from government interference and can publish whatever it likes to publish, I don't think the media is particularly objective or independent. But independent and objective media is a myth anywhere in the world. Almost all journalism suffers from biases, either institutional or, at minimum, individual, and in a vast majority of the cases, journalism lacks objectivity and has an agenda. It is no different in India.

The past two decades have seen an explosion in print and television media in India, and the jostling for consumer mind space has seen the industry rapidly lower its standards. The media in India has become very trigger happy, and even minor issues are sensationalized by it. Accountability of the media to the public has declined, and trials by media have become commonplace. And since negativity sells, the proliferation of media has made India and Indians (and, as a consequence, the world) very depressed about the current state of India.

The good news from an investor's perspective is that India washes all its dirty laundry in the open. News mongering has made it very hard to keep skeletons hidden in the closet, and what you see is what you get in India. In recent times, media pessimism has overshot, and the reality is probably less bad that what the press would have one believe.

THE ULTIMATE FREE MARKET

In my opinion, India is the ultimate free market. No one runs India. People often joke that the Hindu god Lord Krishna also gave up a long time ago and stopped running India. India is run by 1.2 billion Indians and the millions of micro decisions they make every day. Free markets are messy and chaotic, but like nature, they are inherently self-correcting and have automatic stabilizers.

While India might move in the direction of its true potential in fits and starts and frustrate Indians and foreigners in the process, the likelihood of a spectacular collapse or a revolution in India is extremely low. I am not sure that the same can be said with a similar degree of confidence about many other significant participants of the global economy.

SUMMARY

India's democratic form of government is a unique experiment in the history of the world. India is one of those rare countries in the emerging world where democracy functions effectively and where the will of the people is truly represented in elected government. The confusion that manifests itself in India's elected government is the outcome of the differing needs, aspirations, and voices of its 1.20 billion citizens.

The process of consensus building is well under way in India, and even though it is hard to believe, Indians are very rapidly converging on the direction in which they want their country to go. The fact that India is choosing its development path from the bottom up, instead of having a development path imposed on it from the top down by its leaders, means that its development model will have longevity and sustainability that will outlast most of its peers. The automatic stabilizers built into its form of government and its development model will ensure that the country will probably not suffer from spectacular revolutions or a spectacular collapse. This makes India one of the most attractive investment destinations for generating high rates of return over a very long period of time.

CHAPTER 3

The Economy

India's economy has witnessed many changes in perception and expectation over the decades. In the 1970s and 1980s, India's economy was branded as one that could not exceed the Hindu rate of growth of 3.5 percent due to its socialist orientation. Economic liberalization in the 1990s and the Goldman Sachs BRICs report of the 2000s created expectations that India's economy would converge with China's and experience double-digit growth rates. The aftermath of the global financial crisis and the emergence of India's own policy stagnation has once again put into question India's ability to grow at high rates and has brought out the naysayers who explain away the 9 percent growth rates of the 2004–2009 period as an aberration. The problem has always been with the perception and expectation from India's economy and the comparison with other economies that have very different development models. India's economy is driven by its own unique model and is likely to follow a path that is distinct from any other economy.

OVERVIEW OF THE INDIAN ECONOMY

India is a fairly small economy relative to its size, history, and population. In 2012, India's gross domestic product (GDP) measured $1.80 trillion in nominal terms. Compared with China's GDP at $8.20 trillion, Brazil's GDP at $2.45 trillion, the United Kingdom's GDP at $2.45 trillion, and Russia's GDP at $2.0 trillion, India is an also-ran in the world economy.

Even when one looks at India's other economic indicators, the data are mediocre at best. India's headline inflation rate is in the range of 6.00 percent, and overnight interest rates are at 8.00 percent. India runs a fiscal deficit (Union government and state governments combined) of close to 8.00 percent and a current account deficit of between 4.00 percent and 5.00 percent of GDP.

Given these figures, one wonders what all the fuss is about. I recently met with the CEO of a very large Japanese leasing company that has been

in India for over 20 years and asked him about his experience in India. They
have made no money in India and have not been able to build a meaningful presence for various reasons. I asked him why they do not forget about
India and focus on other markets that are much easier to work with. He
replied that, for them, India was *too big to be ignored.*

The big promise that keeps foreigners coming back to India despite
its miserable track record and frustrating operating environment is a population of 1.20 billion people with demographics that are exciting. More
than 50 percent of India's population is under the age of 25 and more
than 65 percent of India's population is under the age of 35. Until a few
years ago, India's GDP was growing at 9 percent, and optimists enamored
by Goldman Sachs's famous BRICs report hoped that it would converge
with China's double-digit growth rates. However, with the financial crisis and global deleveraging, the dreams of emerging-market convergence
withered away. In fact, India and other emerging markets are back in
crisis mode.

Even though India's GDP is $1.80 trillion and the United Kingdom's
GDP is $2.45 trillion, somehow the Indian economy seems larger than the
United Kingdom's. This has to do with what economists call *purchasing
power parity (PPP).* Things in the United Kingdom nominally cost more
than things in India, and therefore to make an effective comparison of
output, economists adjust GDP to reflect PPP. PPP adjustments are very
unscientific. They also do not take into account vast differences in quality
and the fact that in wealthy countries bottom-of-the-pyramid quality of
goods and services are not even available. On a PPP basis, India's GDP
is $5.70 trillion, the United Kingdom's GDP is $2.38 trillion, China's
GDP is $13.38 trillion, Brazil's GDP is $2.30 trillion, and Russia's GDP
is $2.50 trillion.

TABLE 3.1   Nominal versus PPP GDP

Annual Gross Domestic Product (in US$ billions)

	Nominal	PPP adjusted
Brazil	$2,450	$2,300
China	$8,200	$13,380
India	**$1,800**	**$5,700**
Russia	$2,000	$2,500
United Kingdom	$2,450	$2,380
United States	$15,700	$15,700

TABLE 3.2   Income Comparison of Indian States

S. No.	State	GSDP (US$ billions)	Population (millions)	Per-capita income (US$)
1	Andhra Pradesh	100.35	84.67	1,185.19
2	Arunachal Pradesh	1.53	1.38	1,108.70
3	Assam	19.52	31.17	626.24
4	Bihar	35.60	103.80	342.97
5	Chhattisgarh	23.19	25.54	907.99
6	Delhi*	46.00	16.75	2,746.27
7	Goa	5.46	1.46	3,739.73
8	Gujarat	90.65	60.38	1,501.32
9	Haryana	45.67	25.35	1,801.58
10	Himachal Pradesh	9.14	6.86	1,332.36
11	Jammu and Kashmir	9.13	12.55	727.49
12	Jharkhand	22.46	32.97	681.23
13	Karnataka	70.89	61.13	1,159.66
14	Kerala	48.63	33.39	1,456.42
15	Madhya Pradesh	45.81	72.60	630.99
16	Maharashtra	190.31	112.37	1,693.60
17	Manipur	1.83	2.72	672.79
18	Meghalaya	2.64	2.96	891.89
19	Mizoram	1.19	1.09	1,091.74
20	Nagaland	1.59	1.98	803.03
21	Odisha	34.27	41.95	816.92
22	Punjab	42.11	27.70	1,520.22
23	Rajasthan	53.93	68.62	785.92
24	Sikkim	0.73	0.61	1,196.72
25	Tamil Nadu	97.97	72.14	1,358.05
26	Tripura	3.08	3.67	839.24
27	Uttar Pradesh	109.77	199.58	550.01
28	Uttarakhand	13.14	10.12	1,298.42
29	West Bengal	84.57	91.35	925.78
	INDIA total	**1,800.00**	**1,200.00**	**1,500.00**

*Union Territory. National Capital Region

I prefer using nominal GDP as the benchmark, and on that metric India is a relatively small economy with a lot of potential and promise.

Even within this relatively modest GDP figure, there exist large disparities in per-capita income levels among the various states of India.

This has a tremendous impact on the basic building blocks of society like education, health care, clean water, and sanitation. Large parts of India and large portions of India's population have standards of living that are similar to the poorest parts of sub-Saharan Africa. The concerning part from a development perspective is that most of India's demographic surge has taken place in these poor and illiterate parts of the country. Many economists have referred to the Indian demographic dividend as a demographic time bomb waiting to implode.

The improvement in connectivity between the remote parts of India and mainstream India, first through satellite television and then through mobile phones, has had an unimaginable impact on the poorest parts of India, upgrading their income potential and integrating them into the formal economy.

CASE STUDY: The Telecom and Satellite TV Revolution

Given India's fertile landmass and the consequent history of subsistence agriculture, India comprises thousands of villages and hamlets that are inhabited by between 500 and 1,000 people that are disconnected from the rest of the country. They do not have proper road or rail connectivity, electricity, or proper schools, and they do not have access to even basic health care. Farmers from these villages were at the mercy of middlemen who bought their produce from them, or they had to travel long distances on dirt roads to reach the farm *mandis,* or markets. India's telecom and satellite TV revolution changed everything.

India's first mobile telephony licenses were given out in 1995. Until 2001, India had fewer than 40 million mobile phone subscribers. In 2003, India introduced the Calling Party Pays (CPP) regime that made incoming calls to mobile telephones free. This, combined with a decline in outgoing call rates to less than $0.02 per minute and the development of prepaid plans that required payments of less than $5 per month, unleashed the telecom revolution in India. India today has over 900 million mobile phone subscribers, and almost every part of the country has access to a mobile network. Mobile phone connectivity has transformed life in India's tiny villages and hamlets. It has given them access to market information and has enabled them to get a better price for their produce. It has given them access to timely pest management and disease control information for their farms.

Satellite television through Direct to Home (DTH) satellite dishes has brought the world into tiny Indian villages. Community areas in small villages often run televisions with diesel generators, exposing villagers to life in the world outside. Rising income levels and improved connectivity have implanted the desire for better education and upward mobility in the youth of these villages, and they are rapidly integrating into India's formal economy.

India has been a late entrant into the free market club, and a large part of its economy is still dominated by government-owned companies. How India's economy is currently structured has a lot to do with where it is coming from.

INDIA'S UNIQUE ECONOMIC MODEL AND ITS LEGACY

While the British integrated India and built infrastructure that connected the length and breadth of the country, their policies economically debilitated India. They prevented India from participating in the industrial revolution and maintained it primarily as an agrarian economy and a source of raw materials for their factories back home.

With the exception of a select group of Indian businesspeople who pledged strong allegiance to the British crown, most significant and capital-intensive businesses were owned by the British. However, unlike in places such as Australia, New Zealand, South Africa, and Zimbabwe, where European settlers penetrated the entire fabric of society, in India, small and medium-sized trading businesses were almost entirely owned by Indian businesspeople.

Indians did not really prosper under British rule. Farmers lived in destitution, and jobs were available only at the bottom-most rungs in government and the military.

Therefore, when India won independence from the British in 1947, and when India's government and nation builders looked at the economy left behind, they saw a big vacuum with almost no one in the private sector possessing the capability or the capital to fill it.

In this environment, India embarked on a *mixed* economic model. The government of newly independent India became inward looking and focused on import substitution–led growth as a cure for the alleged import dependence created by the erstwhile colonial rulers. While the inward focus helped India build its core industrial base, the extended exile from international trade made India miss out on the postwar boom in global trade enjoyed by countries like Japan, Germany, and South Korea.

The government created large public-sector undertaking's (PSUs) or government owned companies that focused on developing capital intensive and heavy industries like steel, power, mining, energy, telecommunications, insurance etc. These enterprises succeeded phenomenally and became a magnet for aspiring graduates from India's best educational institutions. The government's commitment to industrialization helped India gain confidence, built depth into its economy and created an enviable talent pool, which in later decades became a rich hunting ground for large industrial projects of private enterprises.

In keeping with Mahatma Gandhi's ethos of self-dependence, the government reserved many sectors of the economy for small-scale industries (SSIs) to encourage first-time entrepreneurs. The government supported SSIs with liberal financing schemes as well as tax breaks. While this worked initially, the restrictions and reservations put on sectors reserved for SSIs were so rigid that they prevented SSIs from ever scaling up and in turn made those enterprises inefficient and noncompetitive. The dream of developing a Germany-like *mittelstand* remained just a dream, as the SSI policy failed miserably in its execution.

The mixed-economy approach helped India meaningfully for two decades after independence. However, India failed to make the transition to a free market economy after this initial period of state dependence. The 1970s were a difficult time for almost all countries around the world. It was a time when socialist thinking was at its peak globally. India took away the wrong message from the success of its state-led economic development model and embarked on a draconian nationalization spree under Prime Minister Indira Gandhi. Large sectors of the economy such as banking, insurance, and coal mining were nationalized and merged into PSUs run by the government.

The 1970s and 1980s were lost decades for the Indian economy. Private enterprise was severely curtailed, and PSUs failed to keep up with the pace of growth that was being experienced around the world at that time. Even though India shut itself off from the rest of the world, its extreme dependence on imported energy (oil) led to a balance-of-payments crisis during the Iraq war in 1990. In 1991, India was forced to liberalize and deregulate its economy, putting back into forward motion the wheel that had been in backward motion since the 1970s.

INDIA'S PUBLIC-SECTOR UNDERTAKINGS (PSUs)

India embarked on its mixed economic model with ambitious five-year plans modeled after the Soviet Union. However, these five-year plans were not implemented with the same intensity of government as the Soviet Union. India created PSUs that were effectively independent corporations under the control of different ministries. While the disproportionate burden of achieving five-year plan targets fell on PSUs, their primary motive and objective was to operate as profit-making enterprises. All subsidies and policy-driven support schemes were taken onto the books of the ministries themselves, and PSUs were spared (for the most part) policy-driven losses.

That is not to say that the PSUs were lean and efficient enterprises like their private-sector counterparts. A large portion of the profits earned by

PSUs were driven by resource monopolies bestowed on them and restrictions placed on potential private competition. This did lead to bloating and inefficiency in PSUs over time. However, the ethos of profit orientation and evaluation of capital investments on economic return criteria ensured that PSUs built themselves into functioning corporations and were not mere policy implementation arms of centralized government (unlike the Soviet Union and China).

PSUs in India come in all shapes and sizes. The first distinction that needs to be made is between those companies owned by the Union government and those owned by state governments. The largest PSUs are owned by the Union government. Each company is run very differently from the other and faces different kinds of compulsions and pressures. Over time, these companies have developed very different characteristics and cultures based on the people who ran them and the ministers who ran their respective ministries.

For example, companies under the Ministry of Petroleum and Natural Gas (ONGC, Oil India, Indian Oil Corporation, GAIL, BPCL, and HPCL) are run very professionally and have deep pools of engineering and management talent. However, at various times, allegations of inefficiency and corruption have been leveled against many of these companies. ONGC Videsh Limited (OVL) a 100 percent–owned subsidiary of ONGC, acquired a majority stake in a Russian company, Imperial Energy, for what is now considered an excessively high price and took a very large write-down. Many times, companies like OVL are forced to undertake noneconomic transactions due to personal agendas of their political masters. The professional management of these companies is often not on board with these transactions but have to comply with the decisions of their political masters.

Reliance Industries built one of the largest single-location complex petroleum refineries in the world by relying on a lot of engineering and management talent from Indian Oil Corporation and BPCL. While one could accuse IOC and BPCL of being inefficient or lacking the agility of their private-sector peers like Reliance Industries, they are differently stable and efficient. Their plans are much longer term and more sure-footed and are guided by the five-year plans put out by the Planning Commission. They are less volatile in their investments and are relatively efficient users of capital.

However, companies under the Ministry of Telecommunications and Information Technology (BSNL, MTNL, and ITI) are among the worst-run companies in the country. They are bloated with excessive manpower, provide poor-quality service to consumers, and are terrible allocators of capital. Part of the problem is probably also that they are in an industry that is changing rapidly and has significant interface with retail consumers. The agility of their private-sector competitors has helped them grow at the expense of these government-owned incumbents.

Even in sectors where PSUs have resource monopolies, there are well-run and poorly run companies. For example, Hindustan Copper, which owns a disproportionate amount of India's proven copper reserves, is run poorly, while MOIL and NMDC, which own a disproportionate amount of the high-grade manganese and iron ore reserves of India are much better run. The untapped potential of some of these government-owned resource companies is evident when one looks at the case of Hindustan Zinc. Hindustan Zinc owns a disproportionate amount of India's proven high-quality zinc reserves, including the famous Rampura Agucha mine in the state of Rajasthan. The company was privatized in 2001, and a majority stake was acquired by Sterlite Industries, owned by billionaire Anil Agarwal. Under private management and aided by a tailwind in international zinc prices, Hindustan Zinc increased in value 40-fold in less than 10 years.

CASE STUDY: National Mineral Development Corporation

National Mineral Development Corporation (NMDC: IN) is India's largest iron ore mining company and is majority owned by the government of India. It is an example of a well-run government-owned PSU that operates for the most part like a private enterprise.

NMDC was set up by the government of India in 1958 to fulfill the unmet need of exploiting the vast iron ore reserves of the country. NMDC owns and operates some of the highest-grade iron ore mines in the world in the state of Chhattisgarh known as the Bailadila mines. It also operates mines in the state of Karnataka. The company was an ordinary PSU with an unspectacular business until the late 1990s. The rapid increase in demand and prices of iron ore built momentum in the company, and the decade of the 2000s saw the company scale up output and become spectacularly profitable.

NMDC went public and listed by accident in 1993, when a minority shareholder sold 1.62 percent shares of the company to the public. However, there was virtually no float and consequently no price discovery in the stock until March 2010 when the government of India sold 8.38 percent of its holding in the company at a price of INR300. The follow-on offer was at the peak of the China-driven iron ore boom, and the stock of the company languished as the Indian economy and Indian markets continued to deteriorate. The funding needs of the government of India forced it to sell a further 10 percent stake in NMDC through an offer for sale to the public in December 2012. This time, the government sold into a very thin and depressed market and managed to get only INR149 for its shares. The stock of the company continued to decline and in the recent past has languished below the offer-for-sale level. It is ironic that just as NMDC has built a strong foundation and an even stronger trajectory for its business, and just as a large amount of float has become available to investors, negative perceptions about India and its government have depressed the stock of the company and made it attractively priced.

NMDC's business is very resilient. Investors erroneously assume that NMDC is exposed to iron ore price volatility and that NMDC is in the iron ore business. NMDC has more than 1.2 billion tonnes of high-grade iron ore reserves compared to its current production of about 30 million tonnes a year. It costs next to nothing for NMDC to actually produce the ore. Its entire business is constrained by the lack of adequate transport infrastructure in India's forest and mining belt in Chhattisgarh, and the logistics of getting its output to market is the key binding constraint for the company.

As the judiciary and the government of India have clamped down on illegal iron ore mining, NMDC has been a net beneficiary. As the country's foremost "ethical" miner, NMDC has been able to operate its mines even when others have been forced to shut down. The ban on illegal mining has made India move in the direction of becoming a net importer of iron ore, and NMDC has been able to move up its pricing from one benchmarked to export parity to one benchmarked to import parity (much higher).

NMDC is very different from Coal India, even though both are PSUs and both are in the natural resource sector. NMDC has been a prudent user of capital and has conserved capital and paid rich dividends. Because of the entrenched resource availability with the company, the company is in a very favorable position to exploit its resources by setting up downstream capacities for steel manufacturing. The company has planned to make significant investments to take advantage of this opportunity. At various times, investors have justified not investing in NMDC by pointing to its government ownership or its exposure to iron ore prices and the Chinese economy or to its digressive plans to set up steel manufacturing.

I am not recommending an investment in NMDC. As a disclaimer, various funds that I advise might at times be buyers or sellers in the stock of NMDC, and I should be considered a completely biased party. However, the reason I am discussing the company and the stock here is to highlight how investing based on generalizations is not a terrific strategy for India.

State government–owned PSUs are relatively smaller in size and vary significantly more in terms of their quality and management. States like West Bengal and Odisha have among the worst-run PSUs, while states like Gujarat and Tamil Nadu have among the best-run ones. The better-run state government–owned PSUs, like Tamil Nadu Newsprint and Papers Limited (TNPL) and Gujarat Mineral Development Corporation Limited (GMDC), are run almost like privately owned companies. They seldom get policy support from the Union government, and when they operate in neighboring states, they are treated like any other private enterprise. Of course, they are under the administration of their respective state ministries, and their board and top management are bureaucrats who change every few years. They are not as agile or innovative as their private-sector counterparts, and they operate within long-term plans that do not change very quickly. However, they are run efficiently and for profit and are relatively sound users of capital.

Ownership of businesses by governments is often viewed with skepticism by investors. In a free market economy, government should set policy and regulations and focus on maintaining a level playing field. Business should be left to private capital and entrepreneurs.

However, where businesses exist in government ownership due to legacy, the analysis can never be binary. For example, Singapore Airlines and Telenor are both government-owned companies. However, no investor in their right mind will eliminate them as potential investment candidates merely because of their government ownership. The skeptics will argue that India is no Singapore or Norway. One could then look at companies like DP World of Dubai, SABIC of Saudi Arabia, or Petrobras of Brazil. In the case of these companies, the picture becomes a little cloudy. Finally, one could look at companies like Sukhoi Company of Russia or China Railway Construction Corporation of China, where the picture becomes completely opaque.

The important takeaway from the preceding discussion is that the reality is often multiple shades of gray and seldom black and white. While PSUs can never be mega value creators like companies run by talented and driven entrepreneurs and management, they can earn significantly high returns on capital with relative stability over long periods of time where they have entrenched positions and are run by reasonably efficient management.

Investors have a love-hate relationship with Indian PSUs. There are many investors who choose never to invest in Indian government-owned companies. In my opinion, one needs to delve in deeper and evaluate the individual shades of gray before making decisions one way or another.

MONSOONS AND WHAT THEY MEAN FOR INDIA

Agriculture makes up only 17 percent of India's GDP but employs 51 percent of its workforce. Forty-six percent of India's land mass is arable, but only 30 percent of its land mass is irrigated. Even the landmass that is irrigated sees improvement in output when it receives additional rain. This makes the agricultural sector and therefore the Indian economy dependent on the southwest monsoon rains.

The problem with the southwest monsoon is that it is extremely erratic and unpredictable. The monsoon usually hits the southern Indian state of Kerala by the first week of June and covers the entire country all the way up to the Himalayas by the end of July. The rains continue with full intensity until the end of August, start to taper in the beginning of September, and end by the first week of October. Well, that is what the doctor ordered. However, the monsoon seldom follows this pattern. In some years, the monsoon sets in early with heavy intensity, flooding the country and damaging crops, only to completely disappear in July and reappear tentatively into the following months. In some others, it sets in very late and does not precipitate adequately, thereby causing the soil to lose much-needed moisture. The monsoon can sometimes cause floods and at other times cause droughts, and sometimes cause floods and droughts in different parts of the country at the same time. The monsoons can be normal or above normal for many years consecutively and can fail or be below normal for several years consecutively.

The impact of the monsoon rains on the Indian economy is far greater than the 17 percent of GDP that agriculture represents. A plentiful monsoon ensures sufficient storage in the country's water reservoirs and keeps food price inflation under check by producing a bountiful harvest. A good harvest puts money in the hands of farmers that helps them repay loans and creates rural demand that keeps the entire economy in motion. Absence of farmer distress in the hinterland keeps political masters at ease and allows them to (potentially) make policy decisions that are controversial. It also alleviates the pressure to give handouts and support to farmers and eases pressure on government finances.

The importance of the monsoon to the economy and hence to the financial markets makes all economists and investors monsoon watchers heading into May every year. In years when the economy is on edge and the macro conditions of the country are delicately poised, a poor monsoon can have a devastating impact on the economy.

The fact that 66 years after independence the Indian economy is so heavily dependent on the monsoons is a testimony to the failure of successive elected governments. The few dams that have been built by the government with their allied canals and infrastructure have been roaring successes. It is surprising that the government has not attempted building more of them. The most recent dam built in India was the Sardar Sarovar dam on the river Narmada in the state of Gujarat. The project was conceived in the 1980s and became mired in controversy that stalled the project in the 1990s. A landmark judgment by the Supreme Court of India in 2000, combined with the indomitable will of Gujarat chief minister Narendra Modi, led to the completion of the most critical features of the dam and the canal network. The dam changed the agricultural landscape of Gujarat and rehabilitated the arid regions of Kutch and Saurashtra in the state.

India is blessed with perennial rivers in almost all parts of the country. Many parts of the country routinely suffer from floods in the rainy season, and many others routinely suffer from droughts. Interlinking of rivers in the north and east of the country and those in the center and south of the country and then connecting the two systems by a north-south canal system is something that has been under consideration and discussion for some time. A project of this magnitude would cost hundreds of billions of dollars and bring a significant percentage of India's landmass under perennial irrigation. It would result in the production of more than 30,000 megawatts of hydroelectricity and would spur the construction industry of the country, creating a gigantic multiplier effect. Interlinking of rivers would also make inland water transportation a viable option. However, a project of this nature requires political will that is completely absent in the current or any foreseeable potential leadership in the country.

CASE STUDY: Delhi and the Yamuna River

The delivery of public goods in India has been a colossal failure. Skeptics argue that interlinking of rivers, irrigating monsoon-fed agriculture and providing health, clean water, and sanitation to rural India are pipe dreams when the government cannot take care of its most invaluable resources right in the national capital.

The Yamuna is the largest tributary of the Ganges and originates in the Himalayas. Until about 100 years ago the water of the Yamuna was clear blue, and it was one of the cleanest rivers in the world. The cities of New Delhi and Agra are built on the banks of the Yamuna, and the world-famous Taj Mahal overlooks it. The rapid growth of New Delhi and towns in Haryana have completely destroyed the Yamuna river. New Delhi discharges about 3 billion liters of sewage every day into the Yamuna, most of it untreated (hotly debated). This has caused the waters of the Yamuna to stop flowing and has made it stagnant for nine months of the year.

Despite numerous debates in Parliament about the condition of the Yamuna, very little has been achieved on the ground. I am an optimist. I believe that the sensitization of the voting public to concerns like the Yamuna will in the not-too-distant future force elected representatives to work on fixing such problems. The good news is that most issues facing India can be fixed with strong leadership. The world has the technology, capacity, resources, and desire to help India fix and build its public services and infrastructure. I believe that building India's public services and infrastructure is one of the biggest impending opportunities in the world today.

THE PROBLEM OF INDIAN AGRICULTURE

Agriculture in India over time has become an unprofitable business. As costs have escalated and selling prices have remained under pressure, the economics of small-lot cultivation has become negative. Farmers are stuck in debt traps, and farmer suicides have become a common occurrence. Erratic monsoons and volatility in the prices of agricultural produce has made life difficult for the average farmer.

Unscientific and politically motivated government distortions of the market mechanism have created imbalances in the agricultural factors of the country. The government has kept the price of urea (a nitrogenous fertilizer) artificially low, while it has allowed the price of DAP (diammonium phosphate, a phosphatic fertilizer) to fluctuate in line with international prices. This has made the spread between prices of urea and DAP artificially large, encouraging farmers to use a dangerously high amount of urea relative to DAP. This distortion alone has started tilting the nutrient balance of India's soil and has a poor long-term prognosis.

The government sets minimum support prices (MSPs) for many crops, especially cereals like paddy and wheat, to ensure adequate production and to "safeguard" farmers. Unfortunately, this results in excessive production of cereals at the expense of other, more needed crops. The government procurement program also places an unnecessarily heavy burden on the government's finances and a large portion of the procured cereals are either stolen or wasted.

While it is important for the government to ensure minimum support to farmers to prevent market failures and avoid rural distress, the process is politically driven, and its main objective is diluted in its implementation. The development of market-oriented safeguards like crop insurance and forwards and futures markets has been halfhearted and slow to take off.

The economics of agriculture globally are moving in the direction of mechanized and large-scale farming. Let's look at the sugar industry in India and Brazil. India produces 24 million tonnes of sugar from 12.5 million acres under cultivation, while Brazil produces 30 million tonnes of sugar from 19 million acres under cultivation. But that is where the comparison ends. The sugar industry in India employs 2 million people compared to 500,000 people in Brazil. The average size of a sugarcane farm in India is 5 acres compared to the average size of 100 acres in Brazil. The smallest farms in India measure about 2.5 acres, and the largest measure about 10 acres. The smallest farms in Brazil measure about 10 acres, and the largest measure about 250 acres. Some companies in Brazil operate farms as large as 25,000 acres. The average size of a sugar mill in India is 3,200 tonnes crushing per day (tcd) compared to the average size of 9,500 tcd in Brazil.

In Indian states like Punjab and Haryana, where average land holding sizes are larger, where irrigation infrastructure is sufficiently built, and where farmers participate in pooled mechanization programs, the income levels of farmers is high and they enjoy a relatively higher standard of living than farmers in the rest of the country. Farmers in these states are also relatively more open to ideas like corporate farming and long-term contract farming.

As India has continued to urbanize and as income levels in rural areas have risen, India has suffered from chronic food price inflation. This is driven by a complete absence of reliable and high-quality supply-chain infrastructure as well as regulatory distortions in trading and intermediation of farm produce. Only integrated supply chains with large capital investment can ensure supply in adequate volumes and lower average unit prices of produce sold to end consumers. The kind of investment needed cannot be made by the government or by individual farmers and traders. Infrastructure of this kind is also unviable on a user fee model. Globally, this kind of infrastructure is built for captive use by large distributors and retailers. The fear of letting large global retailers into the Indian agricultural supply chain has kept the sector mired in controversy. Domestic business groups like Reliance and Bharti are working on building agri supply chains to benefit from this opportunity, while foreign companies like Pepsico and McDonald's are working on bringing their global supply-chain models to India to ensure sourcing of consistent produce at a consistent prices for their India operations. However, the sector needs to open up more, and participation needs to broaden out for there to be a meaningful impact on India's economy. This is an impending and inevitable change that will create large potential opportunities in India.

CASE STUDY: Sugarcane versus Oil Palm

The desire to insulate farmers from the vagaries of the market and to provide them with assured selling prices has overshot to an extreme. This becomes a problem where the government is not the buyer and the final eventual arbiter is the market. This is the situation with sugarcane farming in India. Sugarcane is a water-intensive crop and competes with paddy (rice) for farm space. Once harvested, the juice from the sugarcane stick starts to dry up, eventually rendering the crop unusable. Therefore, sugarcane is cultivated around sugar mills and vice versa. As soon as sugarcane is harvested, it is taken to the mill for crushing.

Cyclicality in the sugar industry is induced by the government's ever-rising support prices for the purchase of paddy and politics around "advised" (mandated) purchase prices of sugarcane by the Union as well as state governments. In years when the price of sugar falls, mills stack up large payment arrears to farmers, and in years when the price of sugar rises dramatically, mills make windfall profits without any benefit to farmers. Several expert committees have recommended that the government dismantle the current methodology of cane procurement and pricing. It has been suggested that the price paid for sugarcane should equal a certain percentage of the price of sugar in the previous season. For example, the price paid for sugarcane could be 70 percent of the price of sugar from the previous season. Therefore, for sugarcane that has a 10 percent yield, the price of a tonne of sugarcane would equal 7 percent of the price of sugar from the previous season.

This pricing methodology has been successfully implemented in the case of the oil palm industry in India. The oil palm tree has a gestation period of three years from the time it is planted to the time it produces its first fruit. The fruit of the oil palm tree comes in bunches known as fresh fruit bunches (FFBs). The FFBs yield about 18 to 20 percent crude palm oil when crushed. The FFBs need to be crushed soon after harvest; otherwise, their oil content deteriorates in quality. Mill owners, farmers, and the government of India have arrived at a formula that is beneficial for all parties involved. Mill owners pay farmers between 13 and

14 percent of the price of crude palm oil, as declared by the government for FFBs. If the mills are able to achieve a yield of 18 percent, then the cost of FFBs per tonne of crude palm oil works out to about 75 percent of its selling price.

Development of innovative contract farming models that take into account the interests of farmers as well as companies are essential for the increase in agricultural productivity and farm incomes in India.

MANUFACTURING IN INDIA

Manufacturing and industry comprises 26 percent of India's GDP and employs 22 percent of its workforce. For a country with a population of 1.20 billion people and a per capita income that ranks 140th in the world, India has not been a source of cheap labor and has failed to build a manufacturing base of the kind seen in China.

There are several factors at play that have prevented the development of the industrial sector in India. India is not a single common market. The distortions in interstate commerce and the cascading impact of duties and taxes results in the fragmentation of manufacturing capacity catering to the domestic market. The proposed implementation of the unified goods and services tax (GST) seeks to address this shortcoming, but the process has been trapped in stakeholder bickering in the absence of strong leadership in the Union government.

The mobility of the labor force in India is low, and large-scale migration is still mired in politics, 66 years after independence. The underdeveloped states of India are Bihar, Uttar Pradesh, Odisha, and the northeastern states with significant surplus labor. The industrially developed and growing states of India are Gujarat, Tamil Nadu, Maharashtra, and Haryana. While the Indian Union is not as divided as the European Union, it is not as integrated as the United States. States in India are divided along linguistic heritage, and inhabitants of different states can be identified distinctly. Large-scale presence of migrant workers in states like Maharashtra and Tamil Nadu involves a delicate balancing act, and the migrants are always on edge. Every now and then, politics causes the presence of migrants to flare up into a protest or controversy and creates a great degree of unease among the "guests." Permanent relocations of migrant labor with family, kit and caboodle, is still not the norm, and there exists a very large remittance economy of migrant workers sending money back "home" to their families. The absence of large-scale migration keeps the labor markets in India distorted and operating below potential.

The labor and democracy nexus keeps large-scale labor employment hostage to destructive policies and trade unionism. Labor laws in India encourage diseconomies of scale. The larger the labor force, the more rigid and inflexible the labor laws. For large-scale employers, there is virtually no exit mechanism, and a business cycle downturn virtually guarantees debilitating losses or bankruptcy. Firing troublemakers or unproductive employees is an impossibility, and large labor forces inevitably tend toward mediocrity and inefficiency. The result is that most large companies and brands prefer outsourcing manufacturing overseas so that they can retain the flexibility of ratcheting up or down sourcing of products depending on market conditions. Unfortunately for the country, rigid labor laws harm the very workers they are designed to protect by keeping total employment far below potential. While there has been a lot of talk about reform of labor laws, given vote bank politics and an absence of strong leadership in the Union government, there has been no action on that front.

The lack of adequate infrastructure keeps costs for industry high and incentivizes imports over domestic production. The absence of sufficient, affordable, and high-quality electricity creates a drag on manufacturing in the country. Poor-quality and inadequate transportation infrastructure keeps the cost of transportation within the country very high. Absence of a component ecosystem creates a chicken-and-egg problem that forces manufacturers to depend on imported raw materials and components, putting them at a disadvantage relative to other countries.

Manufacturing and industry are capital intensive and suffer from start-up inertia. Development of a manufacturing ecosystem usually requires a trigger. This can sometimes be driven by policy and incentives, sometimes by market demand, and sometimes by serendipity and animal spirits. Post-independence India implemented policies that encouraged import substitution. Antitrade philosophy in India heightened in the 1970s and 1980s, creating dramatically lower standards of living and a severe balance-of-payments crisis. In the 1990s, India encouraged exports by providing tax breaks and export incentives. However, in the 2000s, Indian policy makers overdosed on free-trade Kool-Aid and not only withdrew all incentives for exports but moved toward stepchild-like treatment for it. Not only did they damage the country's exports, they also gifted away a large emerging domestic market in sector after sector to foreign manufacturers via exports. The lobby of consumers and importers became stronger than the lobby of manufacturers and exporters, and the country's trade deficit started to widen with a hollowing out of the country's manufacturing.

The explosive growth of India's telecom industry has been a global success story of the previous decade. However, the entire telecom infrastructure of India was built with imported equipment, and India did not use the size and potential of its home market to its advantage. India imports electronic equipment worth $30 billion a year, third only to oil imports of

$100 billion and gold imports of $60 billion. It is expected that electronics imports will surpass imports of gold and oil in the next decade. The lack of a concerted policy to encourage domestic manufacturing and sourcing of electronic equipment has prevented the development of a component ecosystem that creates a very big chicken-and-egg problem for potential domestic manufacturers. The process of open tendering and favoring the lowest-cost bidder combined with mercantilist dumping of exports by countries like China and Taiwan prevents the development of an electronics manufacturing industry in India. For electronics manufacturing to truly take off in India, policy makers and consumers have to be willing to live with higher price of equipment in the short and medium term as the industry builds out and competition sets in. In time, the manufacturing ecosystem could become a potential export contributor to India's economy. Policy makers have made a lot of noise about encouraging domestic manufacturing, but short-term compulsions have short-circuited any potential action on the ground.

Manufacturing in India has done well where cost is not the only consideration. Engineering-intensive industries like auto components, automobiles, power equipment and the like have done well in India. Even here, the advantage of having a large home market is an important consideration. For example, WABCO India is a subsidiary of WABCO Holdings of the United States, formerly known as the Westinghouse Air Brake Company. WABCO has plants in the United States, western Europe, eastern Europe, China, and India. Outside of the United States and Europe, the only engineering research center the company has is in Chennai, India. The Chennai research center works very closely with the research center in Hannover, Germany in the development of products and systems for all of WABCO's plants around the world. Products produced in WABCO's Indian factories are significantly cheaper and of equivalent quality than those produced at any of its other plants. However, WABCO has been slow at transferring manufacturing from its global plants to India. Its plants in India primarily manufacture only those products that are sold in India. It therefore exports from its Indian plants only those products that are sold in India. Globally, WABCO is a leader in antilock braking systems. The Indian government was supposed to make it mandatory for all commercial vehicles in the country to have antilock braking systems. However, the implementation has been much slower than expected. Had antilock braking systems grown in India and become a significant part of WABCO's business in India, it is likely that economies of scale would enable its India factories to become global sourcing hubs for antilock braking systems. But in the absence of growth in the home market, the manufacturing outsourcing story from WABCO's India factories remains significantly below potential.

An example of how animal spirits create a manufacturing ecosystem can be seen in the case of Renault-Nissan's investment in India. Lured by the promise of a large domestic car market, Renault's top management decided that they could not ignore and miss out on a presence in India. Despite the numerous hurdles involved, Renault has invested $2.50 billion in India. However, the promise of the domestic market remains unfulfilled for the company. It has failed to capture meaningful market share, and its plant serves primarily as an export base for its sales in the rest of the region. The investment has not been a bad one for Renault, but the original objective has not yet been met. That India is a success story for Renault-Nissan is evident from the fact that the company is in the process of doubling its investment in India over the next five years. In the absence of a global momentum or trend for car companies from around the world to have a presence in India, Renault-Nissan might very well have bypassed investing in India.

India has tremendous manufacturing potential. Manufacturing and industry can be the only meaningful employment generators for India's large workforce. The contribution of manufacturing to India's GDP needs to improve, and the biggest investment opportunities of the next decade in India will emerge from manufacturing and industry. India needs to use its large home market advantage to build a manufacturing ecosystem in industry after industry. It needs to debottleneck and solve many of the concerns of major investors both from within the country and outside to create the momentum that will build and sustain an investment supercycle in the country.

CASE STUDY: India's Chemical Industry

India's chemical industry and its chemical manufacturing ecosystem is one of the biggest untapped investment opportunities in the world. Being a democracy, India has always laid emphasis on the environment, and industrial polluters have not had a comfortable life in the country. Large-scale industrial disasters of bygone years have ensured that the government, industry, and civil society groups are sensitive to potential pollution from factories. The better companies in India employ safety, health, and environment (SHE) practices that are comparable with the best in the world. However, SHE comes at a price. Indian chemical companies are primarily manufacturers of commodity products that are produced around the world and have international benchmark prices. China's presence in the global chemicals market and its complete disregard for SHE has upset the global pricing scenario. Suppliers from India and China compete on an unleveled playing field. Buyers of commodity chemical products in developed markets pay lip service to SHE but choose to buy products from the cheapest source.

Indian companies have struggled to maintain a hold even on their lucrative home market due to the benevolence of the Indian government to imported commodity products. Indian companies, however, have maintained the upper hand in contract manufacturing opportunities. As chemical manufacturing has become expensive in the United States, western

Europe and Japan, and as environmental compliance has become increasingly onerous and unrealistic in these countries, companies have started outsourcing the manufacturing of products to more cost-effective economies like India. India wins over China in contract manufacturing because outsourcers are less worried about the theft of their intellectual property in India and because they are more comfortable with the SHE practices of Indian manufacturers. When buyers purchase bulk commodities on international markets from unknown sellers, they are able to feign ignorance about the conditions under which the products were manufactured. However, when buyers enter into 10- and 15-year contracts for supply of products, they have to be much more diligent about the manufacturing conditions of their suppliers.

India's high-quality and cost-effective engineering talent and capabilities, its protection for intellectual property protection, and its respect for SHE have made India the favored destination for long-term contract manufacturing. This trend is likely to accelerate going forward, and India will become a meaningful player on the global chemical manufacturing scene.

INDIA'S INFRASTRUCTURE DEFICIT

While China's economy is characterized by chronic overinvestment in fixed assets, resulting in oversupply in almost all sectors of the economy, India's economy is characterized by chronic underinvestment in fixed assets and a consequent supply shortage in almost every sector of the economy.

India is a very unpleasant country to live in and to visit. Indian cities routinely rank the lowest on global livability surveys, and a posting to India is considered a hardship posting for expatriate talent. Traveling in and out of India is a nightmare, and only the most driven of individuals choose to make the trip. It is not just in the "optics" that India fails miserably. Industry suffers due to chronic shortages of electricity, roads, railways, ports, airports, water, housing, land, and so on.

Why is India not like China? Why can't India replicate the "build it and they will come" boom that has been successfully experienced in many parts of the world in recent times.

The reason is that in the hierarchy of direct needs of India's overflowing population, infrastructure comes in at the very bottom. Infrastructure's biggest benefit is indirect, and the multiplier effect is an indirect effect. Political expediency and vote bank politics ensure that those who come to power are able to do so on the basis of the most immediate and pressing direct issues, and absence of infrastructure is clearly not one of them. Let us take the example of Mumbai. As discussed in the previous chapter, the Mumbai Metropolitan Region (MMR) has a population of 21 million compared to the population of Maharashtra of 112 million. Of the 21 million people who live in the MMR, a disproportionate number live in shanties and slums. For the slum dwellers of Mumbai and the inhabitants of Maharashtra, the impact of an improvement in the civic infrastructure of Mumbai is an irrelevant outcome. The party or individual that rules Maharashtra is likely to get a lot more political mileage and votes by playing politics with Maharashtra's cooperative sugar industry than by improving Mumbai's civic infrastructure. By the same measure, elections for Mumbai's city council, the BMC, are won or lost based on the mandate of slum dwellers and not the educated citizens who inhabit the city's highrises. The BMC has an annual expenditure budget of $5 billion, making it the richest city council in the country. However, a very large part of that expenditure is wasted on sustaining a bloated employee base and another major part of it is siphoned away by corruption in the award of various contracts. The complete lack of accountability makes the problem continue to fester and grow by the day.

When it comes to building trunk infrastructure like roads, railways, and ports that only the government can build, the political will and monetary resources are completely absent. The Union government runs a large fiscal deficit that is primarily composed of expenditure on salaries; defense; and food, fuel, and fertilizer subsidies. Very little money is left over for fixed-asset investment.

It has been estimated by the Planning Commission of India at various times that between $500 billion and $1 trillion of investment is required for India to bridge its current infrastructure deficit. Since the government does not have the resources for these investments, almost all of it has to come from the domestic private sector and from foreign investment. The government tried to implement a public-private partnership model to attract investment into various kinds of infrastructure in the country. The efforts by the government have failed miserably, and almost all investors in Indian infrastructure have lost money.

There are several reasons why private investment has not been successful in Indian infrastructure. The government did not play its part and did not fulfill its end of the bargain due to an absence of leadership. Highway contracts were awarded by the National Highways Authority of India, but land acquisition was not completed in time in a majority of cases, resulting in project delays, cost overruns, and a complete breakdown of the viability of contracts, which had very little margin for error to begin with. Ultra mega power projects were awarded by the government of India without getting environmental clearance for the plant locations and without providing assurance for fuel linkages. The private sector can bring in capital and execution expertise; however, the government has to play its part in enabling fast regulatory approvals and removing potential roadblocks for the smooth implementation of projects.

High levels of corruption made projects unviable and only those entrepreneurs whose intention was to overleverage and embezzle funds in the construction of assets, with no intention to service or repay borrowings, participated in project bids. At the height of the India investment mania in 2006 and 2007, many infrastructure projects were underwritten at bid values that were likely to generate returns on invested capital that were less than the cost of debt capital. Not only did entrepreneurs get carried away, but the payoff expectations of politicians and bureaucrats went through the roof. Most projects were built on 100 percent leverage with inflated cost projections that involved significant siphoning-off of funds in the construction process. While the party was on, everyone felt that somehow everything would work out in the end. The saving grace was that despite all the shenanigans, some assets were built well and to world-class standards. Several other assets were built so poorly that they will likely have to be torn down in the not-too-distant future. For the well-built assets, there is a future after significant equity and debt write-downs are taken by the original investors.

There is a Gresham's law at work in the interaction between the private sector and government in India. A large number of licenses, concessions, and project awards involve corruption, which results in the incrimination of almost all private entities that undertake any kind of transaction with the government. An inherent suspicion and unwillingness has developed within the bureaucracy, the administration, and the public to let private capital make above-normal returns by investing in anything where the government is a counterparty. The attitude that when one loses money it's their problem, and when one makes money, one has stolen the country's family silver has not been very helpful.

When the savings-and-loan crisis hit the United States in the early 1990s, the Federal Reserve under Alan Greenspan and the U.S. Treasury created the Resolution Trust Corporation (RTC) to liquidate more than $390 billion dollars of savings-and-loan assets and the Resolution Finance Corporation (REFCO) to finance the purchases of those assets. In order to encourage the private sector to participate, the RTC sold assets at fire-sale prices, almost guaranteeing outsized returns for investors. The approach taken by the RTC resulted in quick resolution of the problem and prevented major contagion in the financial system. In hindsight, almost all commentators termed the actions of the RTC a success. The RTC created many millionaires and a few eventual billionaires. Had such a process been implemented in India, it would have become a major scandal, and there would have been many commissions and joint parliamentary committees established to probe for irregularities in the process.

Mega-wealth creates insecurity and distaste in the average Indian. India and Indians have to come to terms with rapid and large-scale wealth creation as a reward for risk taking if the country has to attract the kind of capital and investment needed to upgrade its infrastructure.

CASE STUDY: Delhi Metro versus Delhi Airport

The Delhi Metro and the Delhi Airport are a study in contrast of how infrastructure projects in India have been allotted and built. The Metro was built completely by a special-purpose entity called the Delhi Metro Rail Corporation (DMRC), owned and managed by the government, whereas the Delhi Airport was built under the public-private partnership model. The Delhi Airport was allotted based on open bidding and was won by the GMR Group (GMRI: IN). The Delhi Metro has been hailed as one of India's most successful infrastructure projects ever, while the Delhi Airport has been mired in controversy from the day it was allotted.

The Delhi Metro was built by railway man E. Sreedharan, who had earned his stripes in the implementation of the technically challenging Konkan Railway project of the Indian Railways. Sreedharan maintained an impeccable and corruption-free record in the construction and operation of the Delhi Metro. It has the reputation of being one of the very few urban transit systems in the world to make an operating profit. That an infrastructure project in a country like India could be built within cost, on time, and to world-class standards is a tribute more to Sreedharan than to the capabilities of the government of India. Without exception, government-built projects in India are built below standards, above cost, and with distastefully high corruption.

The fact that the Delhi Metro is an anomaly rather than the norm is why the government of India decided to upgrade the Delhi and Mumbai airports on a public-private partnership model, and rightly so. Winning the bid to upgrade and operate the Delhi Airport was going to be a money spinner at any price. The choice that the government had was to let the Airports Authority of India upgrade and operate the airport and end up with a shoddy asset mired in inefficiency or to hand it over to a private bidder, get a world-class asset, and in the process let the bidder earn an attractive return on its investment. There is absolutely no doubt that there was corruption involved in the award of the Delhi Airport. I don't think GMR had a choice. A project of this nature cannot be won in a country like India without payoffs at the right places. GMR did use its political clout to probably stretch the favoritism shown to it a little too much by shifting the goalposts a little after the award of the contract. Allegations that GMR used loopholes in the Operation, Management, and Development Agreement (OMDA) to reduce its capital commitments and enhance its long-term returns are probably partially true. But that is a function of inexperience on the part of the government in drafting the OMDA and the intelligence on the part of GMR's advisers and management, for which no one can really be faulted. The experience of projects like the Delhi Airport will lead to improvement in bid agreements of successive projects awarded by the government. However, it is inappropriate for the public and the media to embark on a witch-hunt against a private bidder like GMR and to accuse it of profiteering on a government contract. Unlike the DMRC, GMR is a for-profit group, and its objective is to maximize returns to its owners. India and Indians have to come to terms with the fact that unless private investors can participate in government projects and earn an above-normal return, future projects are unlikely to receive any interest from them.

Even though the Delhi Airport project is a high-return project won by the GMR Group, it is unlikely to benefit minority investors in the GMR group. GMR Group companies operate with very poor standards of corporate governance. The majority owners are infamous for padding construction costs and siphoning funds in the construction of their infrastructure projects to the detriment of lenders and minority investors in their companies and projects. Their group companies are also infamous for overleveraging, cross–subsidizing, and opaque dealing across their various projects and assets. What you see is not what you get, and the risks for minority investors in one part of their group to get impacted by problems in another part of the group are very high. Groups and companies like GMR are highly geared to an economic boom and are likely to do exceedingly well at the top of economic and market cycles. However, I do not consider investing in such companies a prudent investing approach in India.

INDIA'S SERVICES ECONOMY

Services make up 56 percent of India's GDP but employ only 26 percent of its workforce. India has an unusually large services sector for its stage of development. India is unique in that it has a fairly large services export sector that is distinct from its domestic services economy. India exports services worth $76 billion a year. These exports create a multiplier effect on the economy and create five indirect jobs for every direct export job. The services export sector has created great upward mobility among urban Indians and led to a meaningful upgrade of Corporate India's work culture and practices. The sector was propelled by a large number of first-generation entrepreneurs with technocratic backgrounds, who created meaningful wealth for themselves and kindled the dreams of thousands of others.

The services export sector in its heyday recorded annual growth rates of more than 30 percent. However, as the developed world economies have slowed down, and as salaries between India and the developed world in the services export sector have started to converge, annual growth rates for the sector have declined to 10 percent. It is relevant to ask whether the sector developed merely because of the arbitrage between salary levels in the developed world and India, enabled by telecom and air connectivity, or whether there was something more fundamental at play. As the slack of high-quality unemployed graduates in the Indian economy has been used up, the sector has been facing significant wage cost inflation.

India produces millions of graduates every year. However, the quality of higher education in India is so poor that most of these graduates are completely unemployable. Many of them are also untrainable and unupgradeable. Given India's demographic surge, there is a very acute need for high-quality education in the country. The education sector presents a very big potential investment opportunity; however, affordability of quality education remains a major challenge. There have been several attempts by entrepreneurs and venture capitalists at starting and funding companies that try to capitalize on the education opportunity in India. Several of these venture capitalist-funded companies have also gone public in recent years. However, almost all of them have failed miserably, and not one of them has been able to come up with a viable business model that bridges the chasm between the need for quality education and the affordability and ability to pay for it.

India has a fairly large financial services industry. I will discuss more about India's financial services sector later in the book. High-growth service areas in the Indian economy include leisure and entertainment, retail, advertising and media, travel and allied services, and transportation and logistics.

INDIA'S NATURAL RESOURCE WEALTH

India is endowed with large and high-quality mineral resources. However, India is a net importer of natural resources primarily driven by oil. Almost all of India's mineral wealth is in the forest and tribal belt in the center and east of the country. Exploitation of mineral resources has always existed in India, and since resources are free (cost of extracting them notwithstanding), and since they come out of the ground, they attract local strongmen and often provide a favorable backdrop for political activity.

Established mineral jurisdictions like Australia, Canada, and the United States have clear policies about how to deal with the trade-off between exploitation of mineral resources, the environment, and society. There are things that are acceptable and those that are not, and others that require strict guidelines to be followed. Enforcement of the law is resolute, and individuals and interest groups cannot change the rules at their whim. India has not made up its mind about what it wants to do with its mineral resources. The approach of successive state and Union governments in India has been haphazard and has oscillated with dominant public opinion of any given period. This puts private investment and capital at serious risk and encourages the development of unscrupulous strongmen and politically supported mafias.

An interesting example of how India shot itself in the foot by not having a clear policy on mining is the story of the iron ore industry in India. Iron forms 5 percent of the earth's crust and is one of the most abundantly available minerals in the world. It is also one of the easiest minerals to mine and produce. India has one of the world's largest reserves of high-grade iron ore. No one cared much about iron ore until 2001, when China's production of steel reached a tipping point and upset the global iron ore equilibrium.

China, which is the world's largest producer of steel and the world's largest producer of iron ore, could not produce as much iron ore as it needed for its rapidly growing steel production and started a global scramble for iron ore resources.

The price of iron ore, which had stayed between $10 and $15 per metric tonne for more than two decades, shot up to $30 per metric tonne by 2003/2004 and then to $200 per metric tonne by 2010/2011. Mines in Indian states of Jharkhand, Orissa, Goa, and Karnataka that had been closed for a long time revved back to life. There was a free-for-all as India's exports of iron ore increased from 40 million tonnes per year in 2001 to 120 million tonnes per year in 2009/2010. In value terms, the exports of iron ore increased 10-fold and at its peak brought $15 billion into the country. Since it cost less than $20 per metric tonne to extract iron ore from the ground, there was a gravy train that was exploited by everyone who could. The Indian railways charged $40 per metric tonne for inland transportation of ore from Jharkhand and Orissa to the port for short distances where alternate transport networks were not available. Political strongmen indulged in illegal mining from unlicensed areas without any consideration for the environment and workers.

The speed with which the iron ore industry grew caught the Indian government off guard, and it was unable to effectively regulate it. In this backdrop, public interest litigations in the Supreme Court of India resulted in blanket bans on all iron ore mining in state after state. India's production of iron ore plummeted and iron ore exports collapsed. In a span of three years India became a net importer of iron ore, and $15 billion of foreign inflows into the country disappeared. While it was necessary for the authorities to clamp down on unsustainable mining, it remains a fact that the sudden boom in iron ore created a lot of wealth for people in the iron ore mining chain. One is left with the feeling that at multiple levels within the government, the judiciary, and the public there was a perception that it was unfair and wrong for people to have made so much money in a such a short time for not doing much. But that is the nature of capitalism. It is a duty of the state to protect the wealth of private citizens when acquired by legitimate means with full adherence to the law. India and Indians have not completely made up their minds about this. In the absence of leadership at the very top, myriad opinions and interest groups have taken the country's core ethos hostage to their own agendas.

India's natural resource sector has the potential to attract large investments as well as to generate livelihoods and wealth in neglected parts of the country. The country needs to very quickly frame clear rules of the game and then to scrupulously implement those rules encouraging an environment of risk taking and wealth creation.

CASE STUDY: The New Exploration and Licensing Policy

India is one of the most underexplored hydrocarbon geographies in the world. India is also one of the most disliked hydrocarbon geographies in the world. The country imports more than 80 percent of its crude oil requirements. The need to increase domestic hydrocarbon output has never been more acute. However, the attitude of the government and the bureaucracy has consistently disappointed investors and in many case caused them meaningful losses.

The government of India launched the New Exploration and Licensing Policy (NELP) in 1999 and offered exploration blocks to private bidders under a Production Sharing Contract (PSC) system with the Director General of Hydrocarbons functioning as the regulator. The PSCs involved a cost recovery system that allowed the operator to recover a certain ratio of its investment costs in the block, and only the profits over and above that were required to be shared with the government.

This particular feature of NELP and the bureaucracy of the DGH has derailed the entire exploration and production industry in India over the past decade. Under NELP, operators were required to submit detailed budgets and plans for expenditure on their respective blocks to the DGH and were required to seek its prior approval. Deep-rooted mistrust of the private sector and the lack of capacity within the DGH to quickly evaluate and respond to requests from block operators created a major bottleneck and put exploration and production programs into disarray. Exploration and production is a capital and equipment intensive business that is very sensitive to time delays.

The dispute between the Ambani brothers discussed in Chapter 1 and the mudslinging of younger brother Anil Ambani against Mukesh Ambani led to allegations by him that Reliance Industries had submitted costs to the DGH for its prolific KG-D6 block that were highly inflated. This set the cat among the pigeons, and if there was any benefit of the doubt being given to block operators by the bureaucrats in the DGH and Oil Ministry, it was taken away. Every block operator was considered guilty until proven innocent.

To further exacerbate the situation, there were rumors of a fallout between Mukesh Ambani and the top leadership of the United Progressive Alliance (UPA) government that led to a determined effort on the part of the government to impair the ability of Reliance Industries to generate a return on its exploration and production assets. The acquisition of Cairn India, the operator of the other big hydrocarbon asset in India (the Barmer block in Rajasthan) by Anil Agarwal's Vedanta Group was another soap opera that survived all attempts at derailment by Reliance Industries as well as the top leadership of the UPA government. The government's poor treatment of the Vedanta Group during its acquisition of Cairn India conveyed a very poor message to potential large investors in India's hydrocarbon sector.

In recent months, it appears that the government and the bureaucracy are slowly coming to the understanding that mistreatment of the energy-producing community at the expense of the energy-consuming community is not likely to be favorable to India's long-term interests. An expert committee headed by former Reserve Bank of India governor C. Rangarajan has recommended deregulating natural gas prices and linking it to a market-based formula. The committee has also recommended changing the methodology of the PSC system under NELP to completely eliminate the concept of cost recovery and to link government compensation to output from day one. The DGH also has been taking a less incriminating approach toward block operators.

In my view, India has climbed a very steep learning curve during the past decade, and a lot of lessons have been learned by both investors and the government. India's need for oil and natural gas are increasing by the day, and the inevitability of domestic production cannot be denied. I believe that a lot of the pain is behind, and India's exploration and production industry is likely to produce very attractive investment returns in the future.

SAVINGS, LAND, AND GOLD

India is a high-savings economy. Given India's rich economic history and the volatility endured by its population over millennia, thrift and savings are deeply entrenched in the culture. However, savings have always been directed toward hard assets. The two primary avenues of savings for Indians have been land and gold. The importance of land to Indians was explained earlier in the book. Gold has been a great store of value for Indians, as it has allowed them to save in small or large amounts and has allowed them to keep their savings within their own custody, avoiding the devastating results of confiscation, currency debasement, economic mismanagement, wars, and revolutions. It has also served as a means of capital flight from the country without the capital actually leaving the custody of the owner.

Since consumption has traditionally not been a very high priority in India, savings in India are never meant to be used. Their purpose is to provide security and insurance against bad times for the saver and his or her family. In that sense, India's high savings rate does not really help its economy. All the capital that is invested in gold effectively gets locked away unproductively (or exported), never to be used again. Financial assets have developed as savings options only in the past 100 years, and while a large community of investors in financial assets has developed, it is still not as ubiquitous as would be desirable. In such a situation, India has become dependent on foreign investment and foreign risk capital to finance productive capital formation in the country.

The other aspect of the Indian economy that keeps land and gold favored as savings assets is the existence of a very large black (underground) economy. The desire to evade taxes is universal. In India, the nexus between corruption, election campaign finance, and tax evasion keeps in existence an unreported economy that is estimated as being almost as large as the reported economy. Since land pricing can be very subjective, and since it is very difficult to keep large amounts of physical cash around, ill-gotten wealth almost universally finds its way into land investments. Corrupt politicians and bureaucrats often hold hundreds of millions of dollars' worth of land in pseudo-names or front names. However, since land is not very liquid, the liquid portion of illegal wealth finds its way into gold.

A sustained decline in the price of gold and sustained stability in the economy, with stories of successful and sustained wealth creation in financial assets will be needed to gradually change the mind-set of the Indian saver over time. As India urbanizes and modernizes, conspicuous consumption is becoming acceptable and desirable. Savings for specific future consumption needs such as children's education, children's weddings, and retirement, as opposed to savings just for security and insurance, are encouraging savers to look at financial assets.

THE MACROECONOMY

When one looks at India's macro indicators, the picture is quite ugly. India has run sustained fiscal deficits, which currently exceed 8 percent (combined center and state deficits) of GDP and in prior years have exceeded 10 percent of GDP. The deficits are used to finance wasteful consumption expenditure and subsidies, and very little goes into productive investment. India runs a sustained trade deficit and a current account deficit that in recent years has approached 5 percent of GDP. The trade deficit is exacerbated by India's imports of oil and gold. Indians living and working abroad remit almost $70 billion a year to their families in India or almost 3.8 percent of GDP. Had it not been for these remittances, India's current account deficit would have been significantly higher. India has experienced chronically high inflation that in recent years has consistently stayed above 6 percent a year at the wholesale level. As a result, nominal interest rates in India have remained in double digits and the currency has consistently weakened against the U.S. dollar and other currencies.

In my opinion, the macro picture of India is not as bad as it appears. India is starting from a very low base, and for an economy with its population, demographics, and potential, its macro situation is likely to sustain and improve over time. Almost all of India's fiscal deficit is financed domestically. India borrows very little from overseas at the government level. India's total external debt stands at $390 billion, which is 21.5 percent of India's GDP. Of this, sovereign debt is only $80 billion while the remaining $310 billion comprises borrowings by private entities.

India's current account deficit and balance of payments is financed by a surplus on the capital account. The current account deficit of $90 billion is financed by portfolio investments into equities of about $25 billion a year, foreign direct investments (FDIs) of about $30 billion and year, and investments in private and listed debt of about $35 billion a year. While dependence on capital inflows makes India vulnerable to volatility and periodic risk aversion in global financial markets, the absolute quantum of India's capital needs is not very large. China has consistently recorded FDI inflows of more than $100 billion a year over the past decade. Manufacturing investment in China appears saturated, and there is a very large potential for India to attract significant FDI in manufacturing if the government is able to debottleneck and streamline certain problem areas for potential investors.

Investors have also, in recent times, been concerned about the stability of the Indian rupee and the potential for large translation losses due to potential further depreciation of the rupee. A sudden and sharp depreciation of the rupee versus the U.S. dollar in 2012–2013 spooked almost everyone, and commentators have been confused about the causes of such a move. Many have opined that the government has debased the currency and its purchasing power by running sustained fiscal deficits, with liberal subsidies and handouts fueling inflation in the process. Their contention is that the debasement has been taking place over the past decade and the depreciation of the rupee is a mere catch-up with the debasement, with a lot further to go. I strongly disagree with this line of commentary.

The depreciation of the rupee has nothing to do with the purchasing power of the rupee. On a purchasing power parity basis, the Indian rupee is significantly undervalued relative to almost all other currencies. This is also evident from the fact that the depreciation of the rupee has not had a meaningful impact on the trade deficit and has not seen an unusual boost to exports or an unusual decline in imports. The government has also not debased the currency, as the Reserve Bank of India (RBI) has purchased very little of the government's borrowings by printing money (or monetizing the debt). The government has indeed crowded out private investment by borrowing to fund its deficit, thereby keeping nominal interest rates high.

Inflation in India is a function of strong and inelastic underlying aggregate demand driven by urbanization and upward mobility of the rural population and chronic shortfall in growth of aggregate supply due to policy inaction and policy hurdles. Inflation in India is not a monetary phenomenon, as is clearly evident from the inability of the RBI to rein in inflation by tightening money supply. In fact, in my opinion, inflation in India has been exacerbated by the RBI's tight monetary policy that has choked investment and supply creation in the economy. For its part, the RBI's defense is that in the absence of policy action by the government to trigger a supply response, the RBI has no choice but to destroy high-quality aggregate demand by choking money available in the economy in order to maintain the price level and currency stability.

The exchange rate of the Indian rupee is set by sentiment and capital flows at the margin. In fact, I would go out on a limb to state that most of India's macro challenges are an outcome of poor sentiment and confidence. Strong leadership in government and strong policy action can put into motion a virtuous circle in India that can simultaneously fix the problems of a weak currency, high inflation, high interest rates, inadequate supply, low investment, and low economic growth.

SUMMARY

India's economy is on a different growth trajectory than that of its peers. India's democratic form of government requires that its growth carry everyone along. Its government does not have the ability to distort and control its economy like many others. India will probably not grow at double-digit growth rates like China, but it is unlikely that it will return to sub–4 percent growth rates of bygone decades. India will probably grow at high-single-digit rates for a long time to come, with occasional surprises on the upside and disappointments on the downside driven by the business cycle and the global economic environment. India's growth rates will consistently increase the standards of living of its citizens and will provide a very fertile environment for committed investors to generate above-normal rates of return.

CHAPTER 4

Financial Architecture

India is a trading civilization. Commerce has formed the lifeblood of India for millennia. India and Indians understand capital and risk. Trade needed financing, and in the absence of formal banks, traders and lenders in India developed financing systems based on trust. Over the past 200 years, India has built a sophisticated financial system that is the envy of other developing economies. The depth of India's financial markets provides opportunities for investors to invest in assets with different risk-reward profiles and to participate in India's economic growth.

HISTORY

Banking in its modern form was introduced into India by colonial rulers. The concepts of debt, trust, and contracts, however, have existed in India since ancient times. The best-recorded history of ancient India is from the time of the Buddha 2,500 years ago. The Buddha spoke about the definition of happiness for a householder and stated that when a householder borrows a sum of money to conduct his business, earns a profit, repays his debt, and is left with some money of his own, that is considered one of the kinds of happiness for a householder.

Repayment of debt was considered sacred in Indian culture. In the village setting, one's debt obligations did not terminate at death but continued to burden successive generations. Farmers in India are infamous for committing suicide when they are unable to repay their debt and when they remain indebted even after losing their land and livelihood. In fact, Indian philosophy believes that debt follows an individual even after death and one remains burdened by it in successive reincarnations.

Individual property rights have been recognized in India for thousands of years. There has always been a separation between the property of the state and the property of the individual. The state did not have the right to expropriate the property of the individual at whim.

Although the modern contract law in India is based on English common law and was introduced into India in its current form by the country's British rulers, contracts have existed in India for a long time. In ancient times, a man's word was his honor, and going back on one's word was unacceptable, with dire societal and governmental consequences.

CASE STUDY: Prince Jeta's Grove

During the time of the Buddha, there lived a very rich merchant by the name Anathapindika in the city of Shravasti. Once on a business trip to the nearby city of Rajgirah he heard about the enlightenment of the Buddha and went to visit him. He was impressed by the teachings of the Buddha and became his disciple. After spending a time learning under the Buddha, he felt that his friends and family back home in Shravasti would benefit tremendously from his teachings. He invited the Buddha to visit the city of Shravasti. The Buddha accepted the invitation.

Delighted, Anathapindika returned to Shravasti and started making arrangements for the Buddha's arrival. He needed to find an appropriate place for the Buddha and his accompanying Sangha of monks. The place needed to be near the city so that laypeople could visit it; at the same time, it needed to be away from the noise and hustle-bustle of the city so that people could meditate in silence. He identified a beautiful garden close to the city that was appropriate to build a dwelling place for the Buddha and the Sangha. He inquired and found out that the garden belonged to Prince Jeta, the crown prince of the country.

Anathapindika approached Prince Jeta and told him that he wished to buy the garden from him. Jeta was enraged and said that the garden was not for sale and asked Anathapindika to go away. Anathapindika told Jeta that he was very eager to purchase the garden and asked him to name a price. To discourage Anathapindika from troubling him further, Jeta said that the amount of gold that would be needed to cover every square inch of the garden would be the price at which he would sell the garden to Anathapindika. It was a custom in those days that if someone made an offer and the other party accepted the offer, it was a binding contract. Even the king of the country could not dissolve a contract. Anathapindika immediately accepted Prince Jeta's offer.

Legend has it that Anathapindika had gold coins brought out by the cartloads and started covering the ground of the garden with them. Before the entire garden could be covered, Anathapindika ran out of gold. When Prince Jeta saw the Anathapindika's volition and what he had done, he was intrigued to find out the purpose for which Anathapindika would go to such lengths. When he found out the purpose, he told Anathapindika that the gold already laid out was sufficient and the remaining amount was forgiven as his contribution to the cause. That is why in Buddhist literature, the place where the Buddha gave many of his famous sermons was called Anathapindika's monastery in Jeta's grove to give credit to both benefactors of the monastery.

My friends and family often tell me that I have a single-track mind that looks for the economics in every situation. My big takeaway when I first heard this story was that, if true, there were several things that existed in India 2,500 years ago that make India a very promising destination for investors. The first was that there were individual property rights and that, unlike feudal Europe, there were certain properties owned by the king and princes, and there were others that were not. The second takeaway was the existence of private contracts and the sanctity that was accorded to them both by society and by the government. My final takeaway was the concept of a private transaction for the exchange of property that involved a negotiation, a contract, a payment, and a transfer of ownership.

THE BANKING SYSTEM IN INDIA

India has a well-developed banking system. More than 75 percent of banking assets in the country are controlled by government-owned banks. The country also has a small number of cooperative banks, private banks (old and new generation), and foreign banks. Government-owned banks or public-sector banks (PSBs) were created by the Bank Nationalization of 1969. All PSBs are listed on the country's stock exchanges. However, the government is required to maintain at least a 51 percent ownership in all PSBs by law. Private-sector banks are categorized into two kinds by the regulator. Old private-sector banks are those that existed prior to the Bank Nationalization of 1969 and were not nationalized because they were either very small or were focused on a particular community. New private-sector banks are those that came into existence following economic liberalization. Foreign banks have operated in India through branches for a very long time. However, activities of foreign banks have been strictly regulated and controlled by the Reserve Bank of India (RBI). In 2004, the RBI relaxed rules related to foreign investment in the Indian banking sector, and foreign investment up to 74 percent was allowed in Indian private banks. Foreign banks were also permitted to set up 100 percent–owned subsidiaries in the country.

The ability to open bank branches has been a vexing issue between the banking industry and the RBI. The RBI permits domestic scheduled commercial banks to open branches in Tier 2 and lower cities under the automatic route at will. Bank branches in Tier 1 cities previously required the permission of the RBI. In recent policy announcements, the RBI has relaxed restrictions on domestic banks for opening bank branches in Tier 1 cities and put it under the automatic route. However, the number of branches that can be opened in Tier 1 cities has been linked to the number of branches opened in areas where the bank does not have a presence. Foreign banks have been restricted from opening branches under the automatic route. The RBI gives foreign banks permission to open branches based on World Trade Organization guidelines and on the basis of reciprocity. The desire of the RBI has been to have foreign banks incorporate 100 percent subsidiaries in India, whereas foreign banks have wanted flexibility in operations while continuing to operate through unincorporated branches. The RBI has further relaxed rules for foreign banks to operate in India and has given them identical status as domestic scheduled commercial banks (with a few minor exceptions) if they convert their branches to 100 percent subsidiaries. It must be noted that the privileges of domestic commercial banks bring with them their burdens, including adherence to the two bugbears of the banking system in India, the Statutory Liquidity Ratio and Priority Sector Lending norms.

CASE STUDY: Old Private-Sector Banks

The banking sector in India was completely privately owned until the creation of the State Bank of India in 1955 and the Bank Nationalization of 1969. Some banks were not nationalized, either because they were too small or because they specialized in specific areas or served specific communities. These banks have been categorized as old private-sector banks by the RBI. The old private-sector banks have attracted a lot of investor interest during the past decade.

Although all banks are regulated by the RBI, and the RBI maintains a tight grip on the operations of old private-sector banks similar to the grip it maintains on PSBs, not all old private-sector banks are the same. Some are much better run than others and have much higher standards of governance, higher returns on capital, and better-quality loan books than others. The well-run banks have done very well for their shareholders and have compounded capital at high rates of return over a long period of time.

In recent times, old private-sector banks have attracted a lot of interest from market participants due to the potential for them to be sold either to other domestic private banks or to foreign banks looking to enter or expand their footprint in India. The advantage that old private-sector banks bring to potential foreign acquirers is that they are considered full scheduled commercial banks by the RBI and have large branch networks, with the ability to expand them as needed. For domestic acquirers, the old private-sector banks offer regional footprints, since many of them are geographically concentrated in certain parts of the country.

The only foreign acquisition of an old private-sector bank was the acquisition of The Vysya Bank by ING of the Netherlands in 2002 to form ING Vysya Bank (VYSB: IN). Among domestic banks, Centurion Bank merged with Bank of Punjab in 2005, and the combine was acquired by HDFC Bank (HDFCB: IN) in 2008; United Western Bank was acquired by IDBI Bank (IDBI: IN) in 2006.

Some banks have periodically attracted the interest of market participants as imminent acquisition candidates; they include South Indian Bank (SIB: IN), Federal Bank (FB: IN), Karur Vysya Bank (KVB: IN), and City Union Bank (CUBK: IN). Most of the better-run old private-sector banks trade at between 1.10 and 1.30 times price-to-book value and have returns on equity in the 18 percent to 22 percent range. The probability of an acquirer's paying a significant multiple to book value is low in the current scenario, where restrictions on organic growth are being continuously lowered by the government and the RBI. An acquisition at a price-to-book value of 2.0 would be ambitious and probably the best-case scenario. In my opinion, investing in these banks is a low-risk, low-return proposition with the potential back-ended and free option of a medium return in case they are acquired.

Banks are required to maintain a certain percentage of their deposits and liabilities in government securities or gold. This is called the statutory liquidity ratio (SLR). The SLR has been as high as 38 percent of liabilities and as low as 20 percent of liabilities. It currently stands at 23 percent. Although the justification of the SLR is to maintain adequate liquidity in the system, it is an open secret that the government needs the SLR to fund its large and growing fiscal deficits. As discussed earlier, most of India's deficit is funded domestically. The existence of the SLR plays a very big role in helping the government fund its liabilities domestically. The challenge that the SLR creates is that it forces banks to have large treasury operations. This makes them vulnerable to volatility in interest rates above and beyond the normal asset liability mismatches in their banking operations.

NONBANKING FINANCE COMPANIES

Nonbanking finance companies (NBFCs) are institutions that are usually focused on one or a few areas of specialized lending. They are distinct from banks because they are not allowed to accept demand deposits from the public and are not a part of the payments and settlement system of the country. NBFCs were not a formally recognized sector by the RBI until 1993. NBFCs filled gaps in the financial system that were not serviced by banks. For example, banks did not finance used trucks, whereas NBFCs like Shriram Transport Finance (SHTF: IN) built a multibillion-dollar business financing used trucks.

NBFCs have evolved from informal moneylenders and credit providers that have existed in India for centuries. However, in the 1980s and 1990s, there was a mushrooming of NBFCs. In 1981, there were about 7,000 such companies, and by 1996 there were more than 50,000 such companies. Numerous failures in the sector forced the RBI to recognize the sector in 1993 and to fully regulate it through an amendment of the RBI act in 1997–1998.

NBFCs have played a very important role in increasing the financial inclusion in the country. They were instrumental in building and growing many specialized verticals like housing finance, vehicle finance, emergency personal loans, and so on.

CASE STUDY: Kotak Mahindra

Kotak Mahindra Bank (KMB: IN) is the phenomenal success story of first-generation financial entrepreneur Uday Kotak. Kotak started Kotak Mahindra Finance in 1986 as an NBFC with a focus on bill discounting and trade finance. Kotak Mahindra provided focused and specialized service to traders and businesses at attractive rates by understanding their individual business needs. Banks, however, provided trade finance as one of many other products and did not understand the speed and execution requirements of businesses fully.

With early success in trade finance, Kotak Mahindra ventured into hire purchase and automobile purchase financing. This again was a specialized area that was not receiving the needed attention and focus from banks. Kotak Mahindra continued to grow its retail presence and sought borrowers at a time when banks sat on their backsides and made borrowers who came to them wait indefinitely.

As the capital markets in India started to open up after economic liberalization in 1991, Kotak incorporated separate companies for investment banking and brokerage activities. With further opening up of the financial markets, Kotak set up a mutual fund company and a life insurance company. With increasing investor interest in the Indian markets, Kotak expanded his asset management operations and set up venture capital and private equity funds. Finally, in 2003, Uday Kotak's long-cherished dream of setting up a commercial bank came true when the Kotak Mahindra Finance Company received a license from the RBI to convert into a scheduled commercial bank.

Following conversion to a commercial bank, Kotak consolidated all his companies into Kotak Mahindra Bank and it became one of the foremost new-generation private-sector banks in the country. Kotak Mahindra Bank today trades at a price-to-book value of 4.0 and has a market capitalization of $9 billion. His 50 percent ownership in the bank pegs Uday Kotak's net worth at $4.5 billion, making him one of the richest people in India and the world.

By virtue of being leveraged, NBFCs have been prone to financial frauds and irregularities. Despite stringent regulations, the unbanked nature of India's hinterland makes it repeatedly succumb to Ponzi schemes and their innovative promoters. Despite the better efforts of the regulator and the courts, some of these Ponzi schemes are so well designed that it is very difficult to indict them based on rule and law violations.

NBFCs have been one of the sectors most favored by foreign portfolio investors in India, and several of them have built meaningful businesses by raising foreign equity capital at significant premiums from foreign investors. One of the reasons for this is that, unlike the banking sector, foreign direct investment and foreign portfolio investment in the NBFC sector are permitted by the RBI. Another reason is that NBFCs offer foreign investors the ability to deploy large amounts of capital relatively quickly and offer them a leveraged play on India's economic growth. In my view, the sector is an attractive one but fraught with risks. The economics of the NBFC business are fixed and do not offer much room for improvement (although the downside is fully open). Therefore, the key for investors is to invest in NB-FCs with business models that are likely to remain resilient through vicious market cycles and to invest at reasonable prices. Investing in the sector at premium valuations during times of market euphoria is likely to result in below-average returns in the best cases and significant losses in the worst cases.

FINANCIAL INCLUSION

India's financial system and economy have come a long way since independence. When India became independent, farmers and small businesses had no access to credit, and they were at the mercy of usurious moneylenders and other informal networks. Loans for education were hard to come by, and no one lent to economically weaker sections of society.

The government of India via policy made credit available to India's small-scale industries (now known as micro small and medium enterprises) and farmers. It also made loans available for education and brought low-income groups into the formal credit economy. It nationalized the banking system and mandated banks to lend a certain percentage of their assets to these areas and categorized them as priority-sector lending (PSL). Over the years, this kind of forced lending has garnered a lot of criticism.

Investors often erroneously believe that PSL targets are applicable only to public-sector banks and that as a result of PSL these banks carry large nonperforming loan books. PSL targets are applicable to "all" banks in India uniformly, including foreign banks. There is some relaxation for foreign banks that have a small presence in the country; however, they are not fully exempted from the targets. It is true that since public-sector banks have the largest branch networks in the country, they have access much deeper into the hinterland than private-sector banks. It is also true that they face some compulsions to extend credit in underprivileged areas where they probably would not if operating on purely commercial terms.

State Bank of India (SBIN: IN), together with its subsidiaries, has 13,000 branches in India. The total number of bank branches across all banks in India exceeds 80,000 branches. Still, India has only one bank branch for every 15,000 people. While almost 80 percent of all Indians own a mobile phone, only 50 percent of Indians have a bank account. The challenge with financial inclusion is that the cost of delivery of banking services deep into the hinterland and to the poorest sections of society are uneconomical. Several innovations have been attempted by the RBI and public-sector banks, including low-cost rural branches, no-frills bank accounts, business/branch correspondents, micro-ATMs (automated teller machines), and mobile banking. Many of these have been successful, and many others are works-in-progress.

One of the biggest drivers of the demand for banking services in rural India is the need to transfer or remit money. Migrant workers who work in urban areas or in industrial towns periodically need to send money back to their families in villages. Postal money orders used to be the preferred means of transferring money back home, but it was expensive (5 percent of amount transferred), prone to delays, and often prone to fraud. Carrying cash in person or sending it with friends and relatives on trains and buses was also not a sustainable and preferred method of money transfer. With the advent of core banking and interbranch connectivity, banks enabled migrant workers to deposit their income in no-frills accounts at their place of work and enabled their families to withdraw the money through branches, ATMs, micro-ATMs, or branch correspondents in their villages.

The government of India provides subsidies and handouts to underprivileged sections of society under various schemes. Many of these subsidies are either administered in kind or through intermediaries. In order to encourage financial inclusion and to reduce inefficiency and theft in the system, the government of India has embarked on a direct benefit transfer (DBT) scheme combined with a unique identification system for all residents of the country. The scheme is ambitious and fraught with implementation challenges. The goal is to give each resident Indian a unique biometric identification number and to link each of these individuals to a no-frills or mobile bank account. Subsidies and handouts will then be directly transferred into these bank accounts, eliminating shrinkages and losses in the supply chain. It is expected that the DBT will create demand for bank accounts and will go a long way in improving financial inclusion in the economy.

CASE STUDY: Sahara and Its Microsavings Model

Sahara India Financial Corporation is the largest residual (legacy) deposit-taking NBFC in India, with a deposit base of $3 billion, and the largest Ponzi scheme in operation in the country. It also enjoys the benevolence of Mulayam Singh of the Samajwadi Party, a powerful politician of the state of Uttar Pradesh and a potential king maker in India's fragmented Parliament.

The success of the Sahara Ponzi scheme demonstrates the desperate need for financial inclusion, not just on the credit side but also on the deposit side. Sahara operates a microsavings model through the agent-banking concept. Sahara enables poor farmers and individuals in India's thousands of disconnected and unbanked villages and hamlets to save trivial sums in savings schemes operated by its agent-bankers. Customers can deposit as little as 10 rupees a day ($0.15) with Sahara's agent bankers and have complete flexibility to start and stop and increase and decrease these amounts at will without any consequences.

The money is available on demand with accrued interest at any time to depositors. Over the years, Sahara and its army of agent-bankers have built an impeccable track record of service and trust with depositors. The company has never defaulted on a demand by a depositor, and the word-of-mouth reputation of Sahara is so strong that depositing money with Sahara is considered safer than depositing it with the government.

The need in unbanked rural India is more about saving principal than about earning interest. The ability to safely accumulate trivial savings while having the money available on a rainy day is a service that is greatly valued by farmers who live in modest dwellings with no ability to safeguard anything.

From Sahara's perspective, microsavings are the ultimate finance tool. Savings in rural India consistently grow in aggregate, and because of the fragmented and small ticket size of deposits, the system never experiences a run on it. Although Sahara technically "accrues" interest on deposits, this interest never really gets paid until the depositor asks for some or all of his money back. Those depositors who do ask for their money are promptly repaid in full with a smile, thereby preserving the confidence of others and further reinforcing the Ponzi scheme. In the meantime, Sahara is free to divert these deposits to all kinds of businesses and speculative activities without ever having to repay the principal or interest on them. The regulators and the judiciary recognize the systemic risk posed by Sahara and have been after it, but Sahara has done everything right by the book, and the laws are too weak to incriminate it in any meaningful way.

The Ponzi scheme will end someday, as all schemes must, and at that point it will lead to a colossal implosion that will expose a bankrupt Sahara India Financial Corporation with losses of their life's savings for millions of poor Indians from India's unbanked villages.

Financial inclusion not only requires access to bank accounts and payment systems; it also requires access to credit. The term used to provide small-ticket loans to the poorest sections of society is *microcredit* or *microfinance*. Muhammad Yunus of Grameen Bank in Bangladesh is a Nobel laureate and considered the father of microcredit and microfinance. He was a groundbreaker in making small-ticket loans to the rural poor of Bangladesh. Through his research and work, he discovered that women were better borrowers than men and were less likely to squander away their earnings on substance abuse. He also discovered that lending to communities and groups of women, organized as self-help groups, improved repayment rates substantially. Women in the group would help each other out to meet their repayments if others had difficulty to ensure that the group itself did not get a bad name.

As an instrument of social change and upward mobility, microfinance has been phenomenally successful. Sometime during the past decade, however, microfinance caught the fancy of the private equity industry. The industry applied the lessons it learned from the high-yield industry and came to the conclusion that the while each individual loan was risky, millions of small-ticket loans were in aggregate relatively safe and that the high implied interest rates on the loans would provide high internal rates of return on invested capital even after providing for delinquencies. In my view, this was a big mistake—microfinance is organized charity. It is very efficient organized charity. It uplifts neglected sections of society while helping them retain their dignity and self-respect. Its impact on the economy can be significant over time. Earning an above-normal rate of return, demanded by discerning investors, in today's competitive capital markets from microfinance is a pipe dream.

Microfinance suffers from several problems that make it an unattractive sector for for-profit investors. Although the apparent yields in microfinance are big, the cost of delivery and collection create many problems for the sector. The average loan size for a microfinance loan in India is about $150. The administrative and overhead costs of making loans of this size are prohibitively high. Even though the nominal dollar amounts are not very large as a percentage of loan amount, the costs are high. In order to minimize the cost of administration and overhead, for-profit microfinance companies try to concentrate their loan books and try to make as many loans as possible in a given community, village, or town. This creates a big moral hazard problem for the lenders. When everyone in the community is a borrower from the same lender, it becomes very easy to single out the lender and to make it into the villain. The invariable entry of unscrupulous borrowers and a few unpalatable incidents upset the entire ecosystem. Even with geographic concentration, it is very difficult to lend meaningful amounts to creditworthy borrowers and groups. The pressure to deploy capital and build a large loan book forces microfinance companies to lend to every potential borrower and to become a significant counterparty in an otherwise poor ecosystem. This creates regulatory and government problems for the microfinance companies. In a democracy, votes matter and governments always support the large number of "destitute" borrowers against the shenanigans of the supposedly powerful and usurious lenders. Once borrowers realize that lenders have been pushed into a defensive position, delinquencies start to soar as groupthink and rationalization makes even scrupulous borrowers feel like they have been wronged and that they are entitled not to pay back their loans.

Microfinance, in my opinion, is a great instrument that has caught the fancy of the wrong section of the financial markets and is a story that will most likely end in tears in the not-too-distant future.

CASE STUDY: SKS Microfinance

SKS Microfinance (SKSM: IN) is a stock market story that completely baffles me. The company was founded in 1997 by Vikram Akula and is the largest microfinance company in India. It loans money to rural women to alleviate poverty. It saves them from loan sharks by lending to them at 30 percent per year.

In 2010, the company went public and disclosed a marquee list of investors, including Sequoia Capital, Abu Dhabi Investment Authority (ADIA), Vinod Khosla of KPCB fame, Narayan Murthy of Infosys fame, George Soros, and several other "high-quality" institutional investors.

Before the initial public offering (IPO), the company had a net worth of $190 million, and it raised $140 million in its IPO in 2010, valuing the company post money at $1.40 billion or four times its post-IPO price-to-book value. The market post listing took its stock higher and to a market capitalization of almost $2 billion. The story started to deteriorate almost immediately post-IPO. Large-scale irregularities and losses were discovered in the company, and the stock plummeted 90 percent, leaving it with a market capitalization of only $140 million. Immediately afterward, the company wrote off $250 million of loans, reducing its book value to $65 million at current exchange rates.

What continues to amaze me is that the company still has a market capitalization of $300 million at current exchange rates and continues to trade at a price-to-book value of 5. This is a company that is headed to bankruptcy in a hurry and is likely to end up with a negative book value with total losses for equity and debt investors. The objective of microfinance as organized charity will have been served with contributions from financial investors who have done well for themselves in other spheres of their lives and can probably afford a little bit of social contribution from their pockets.

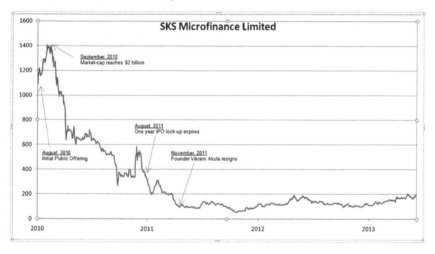

THE RESERVE BANK OF INDIA

The banking sector in India is regulated by the RBI and the RBI has done a commendable job of maintaining the stability of the banking system through several spectacular booms and busts over the decades. The RBI is a conservative regulator and has maintained tight controls on the country's financial system under the pretext of maintaining systemic stability. Under the leadership of previous governor Subba Rao, the RBI regressed due to his incomplete understanding of the monetary system and due to his textbook orthodoxy. Under the current governor, Raghuram Rajan, it appears that the RBI is slowly changing its approach toward the Indian financial system and is working toward liberalizing it and integrating it further into the global financial system. Further integration will obviously make India's financial markets more correlated to global events and will make the country more vulnerable to external shocks. The justification one could provide for further financial liberalization is that there is no shelter from the impact of global financial events anyway, and India is probably much better off being aligned with the global flows of capital in both directions.

The RBI is like a clean lotus growing in the muck of India's politics and bureaucracy. It is a spotless organization that is completely meritocratic and professional and does not experience corruption at any level. The RBI is rightly credited with relentlessly pushing for change and adoption of new technologies in India's financial system and for achieving it incrementally over time. In the early 1980s, the RBI mandated the introduction of magnetic ink character recognition technology on checks and for check processing. In the late 1980s, the RBI embarked on a program for the computerization of bank branches. By the end of the 1990s this program had become mandatory in public-sector banks. By the end of 2009 almost 95 percent of all public-sector bank branches in the country were computerized. In the 2000s, the RBI encouraged the introduction of core banking solutions in public-sector banks that enabled interconnectivity between all branches and enabled real-time transactions.

Although ATMs were first introduced in India in the early 1990s, they really started mushrooming in the early 2000s. By 2005 India had about 16,000 ATMs in operation. In 2007, the RBI in one fell swoop changed the complete momentum of ATM deployment in India. It mandated by policy that ATMs could not charge usage fees on debit cards of other banks up to the first five transactions every month. Thereafter, it capped the usage fees at INR20 per transaction (about $0.30). Similar to how the introduction of the Calling Party Pays regime lead to an explosion in the mobile phone industry, the elimination of ATM usage charges on customers of other banks lead to an explosion in the usage and deployment of ATMs. India today has more than 120,000 ATMs in operation, and their deployment is growing at a compounded rate of 25 percent per year. ATMs have improved in sophistication; however, low-cost rural ATMs have been developed and deployed. The RBI has introduced the concept of white-label ATMs, which are nothing but outsourced ATMs run by third-party operators for a fee. The growth of white-label ATMs, especially in rural areas, is expected to have a significant impact on financial inclusion.

The RBI has worked hard on the automation and improvement of payment systems in the country. The computerization of banks and introduction of core banking solutions was the first step in moving the country toward a robust electronic funds transfer system. To this end, the RBI introduced two electronic payment systems in the country: Real-Time Gross Settlement (RTGS) and National Electronic Funds Transfer (NEFT). The difference between the two systems is that RTGS is processed in real-time settlement between two banks and is meant for high-value transactions over INR200,000 ($3,300) whereas NEFT is processed in hourly batches and is meant for low-value transactions. Once again, the RBI encouraged the widespread usage of RTGS and NEFT by forcing banks to reduce usage charges by statute. The RBI has also strengthened the credit card infrastructure of the country and has introduced several security measures for improving the security of physical as well as online use of credit cards.

Another successful effort of the RBI was the development of the domestic credit rating industry in India. Pradip Shah, the founder of Credit Rating Information Services of India Limited (CRISIL) is truly the father of the domestic credit-rating industry in India. Shah founded CRISIL in 1987 and was a little ahead of his time. However, with the onset of economic reforms in 1991, the recognition of the importance of high-quality independent credit research and evaluation had become pervasive. To the RBI's credit, once the recognition set in, it moved very quickly to establish the rules and regulations around credit rating in the country. India is one of the very few developing countries in the world with a strong and well-developed domestic credit-rating industry. In fact, the strength and depth of India's domestic credit-rating industry has been a springboard for the development of the outsourced financial analytics and credit research industry in India. While I am not a big fan of credit ratings by themselves, the independent research conducted by credit-rating agencies adds a dimension of stability to the financial system.

CASE STUDY: CRISIL

Until India started liberalizing its economy in 1991, its financial markets and regulations were very rigid. There was very little that could be achieved by innovation and entrepreneurship. Tenacious entrepreneurs in India, however, did not stop trying and pushed forward despite resistance. Once the regulators changed their minds and started opening up the system, Indian entrepreneurs caught a tailwind and the speed of change in the Indian markets skyrocketed.

The credit-rating industry in India was a big beneficiary of this evolution. Pradip Shah, who is an alumnus of the Harvard Business School, started Credit Rating Information Services of India Limited (CRISIL: IN) in 1987. The company struggled in its initial years in the absence of a debt market and lack of understanding of the need for independent credit ratings. By 1992, CRISIL's reputation and an independent agency with strong technical skills and rigor was established. In 1993, CRISIL came out with an IPO into a roaring bull market. In 1994, R. Ravimohan took over as the managing director of the company, and a new phase of growth in the company began.

India has a very strong talent pool of chartered accountants and financial analysts. Books of Indian companies are also, on average, better kept and more real than almost all other developing countries in the world. Unlike almost anywhere else in the world, the Indian credit-rating industry is completely built on Indian talent and management. In 1996, Standard & Poor's (S&P), one of the largest ratings agencies in the world, recognized this strength and entered into an alliance with CRISIL that was followed by a minority equity investment of 10 percent in the company the following year. As the credit-rating industry in India grew and as companies like CRISIL scaled, they realized that India had so much high-quality surplus talent that they could service the analytical and technical needs of ratings agencies and other financial services companies around the world. CRISIL built a significant analytics and research outsourcing business and in 2005 acquired Irevna to augment its capabilities. In 2005, S&P acquired a majority stake in CRISIL, culminating a long period of courtship.

Companies like CRISIL with unique businesses and business models have been big wealth creators in the Indian markets. When CRISIL went public in 1993, it raised a modest sum of $1.65 million (at today's exchange rates) at a post-IPO market capitalization of $5 million, and has never raised another dollar of equity since. In 1997, when S&P acquired a 10 percent stake in the company, its market capitalization was $28 million, and by the time it took majority control of the company in 2005, CRISIL's market capitalization had grown to $85 million (at today's exchange rates). Today, CRISIL is a significant business in S&P's global operations and commands a market capitalization of $1.2 billion.

Indian nominal interest rates are significantly higher than those in the United States. Indian overnight interest rates average around 8 percent, while U.S. overnight interest rates are near zero. In such a scenario, a large potential exists for domestic borrowers to borrow in foreign currencies at lower nominal rates while leaving their currency exposure unhedged. There also exists a large potential for leveraged foreign investors to create a carry trade whereby they borrow cheap in foreign currencies and invest in India at high nominal rates, hoping for stability or even appreciation of the Indian currency, enabling them to earn an attractive return. The traditional view of the RBI has been that such hot flows of money that are leveraged and short term in nature create systemic risks for the Indian debt and currency markets. Therefore, the RBI has placed strong restrictions on borrowing by Indian entities in foreign currency and leaving exposures unhedged. The RBI has also kept a tight lid on investments by foreigners into the Indian debt markets. The emerging view under the new RBI governor, Rajan, is that as long as the investor invests in an Indian rupee–denominated instrument, the foreign currency risk is entirely borne by the investor and the risk to the system is not excessively high. The view is that this broadens and deepens both the Indian debt and currency markets. The RBI has therefore slowly eased restrictions on foreign portfolio investment into rupee-denominated debt and has indicated that there is more reform to come. Foreign currency borrowing by Indian entities continues to remain restricted and is unlikely to see significant relaxation anytime soon.

The RBI has managed India's balance of payments well through a very turbulent period in the past two decades. In 1991, India airlifted 67 tons of gold to pledge as physical collateral for a $2.2 billion emergency loan from the International Monetary Fund. This was the event that took India to the brink and triggered its economic reforms and liberalization. From there, the RBI has gradually built up India's foreign exchange reserves that today stand at $300 billion. The reserves are not a panacea in themselves and carry a significant cost for the RBI and the government of India. In the absence of monetization, purchase of foreign currency to add to reserves makes the RBI create a reverse carry trade. The RBI borrows rupees from the market at nominal Indian interest rates and pays it to sellers of foreign currency. It then invests this foreign currency in sovereign debt of the respective foreign countries at nominal rates that are significantly lower than India's. If the rupee remains stable, the loss or the cost of carry to the RBI is equal to the difference in interest rates between the two currencies. That is the theory. In reality, the reserves have built up over time, and the RBI has not had to borrow the entire equivalent amount of its foreign exchange reserves from the domestic market, which means there has been gradual monetization of these reserves. In the heady days of 2006 and 2007 when India was receiving record inflows, the RBI did resort to these borrowings, also called sterilization, by the issue of market stabilization scheme (MSS) bonds.

The RBI does not peg the value of the rupee to any currency or to any basket of currencies. The RBI follows the policy of "managed float" for the Indian currency. The rupee is freely traded in the normal course, and the market sets its price. The RBI intervenes by buying or selling foreign currency only during periods of excessive stress in the system or to smooth out excessive volatility. However, at times, the RBI has taken strong directional views and tried to defend levels in the rupee, sometimes unsuccessfully. In 2007, when capital was gushing into India, the RBI drew a line in the sand at an exchange rate of 39 rupees to a dollar. It did this by buying the excess supply of foreign currency and sterilizing the corresponding liquidity created by issuing MSS bonds. In 2013, India saw large outflows of capital from the country and the rupee plummeted to an exchange rate of 68 rupees to a dollar. The RBI has indicated that it would like the rupee to stay below 60 rupees to a dollar and has tried to defend it by using multiple tools in its arsenal. The existence of a large offshore dollar-rupee market called the Nondeliverable Forward (NDF) market complicates the management of the rupee for the RBI.

CASE STUDY: The FCNR (B) Free Lunch

India is a country that depends on capital inflows to bridge its current account deficit and keep its balance of payments in equilibrium. The complete stagnation of policy making and numerous scandals in recent years have destroyed business and investor sentiment in India and completely stalled the investment cycle. In this backdrop, talk of a withdrawal of stimulus by the U.S. Federal Reserve Bank spooked markets and resulted in a sudden flight of capital from the Indian equity and debt markets. This put severe strain on the Indian rupee and it depreciated by 25 percent versus the U.S. dollar in the span of a few months.

India has always treated its overseas diaspora with care, as they are big source of remittances and capital for the country. Nonresident Indians (NRIs) can invest in foreign currency deposits at favorable rates on a completely tax-free and full repatriable basis. These deposits are called FCNR (B), or foreign currency nonresident (bank) deposits. To bridge the sudden shortfall in the availability of dollars without resorting to sovereign borrowing, the RBI opened an arbitrage window that provided a free lunch for NRIs.

In September 2013, the RBI opened a special swap window for banks and offered them a fixed U.S. dollar–Indian rupee swap at 3.5 percent for funds brought in through FCNR (B) deposits with a tenor of more than three years. The market rate for a similar swap was approximately 7 percent, and the RBI in effect offered a subsidy of 3.5 percent to banks to garner FCNR (B) deposits. The banks in turn passed on some of this benefit to depositors create a gravy train for them in the process. For three-year fixed and irrevocable deposits, banks offered NRIs a deposit rate of 4.7 percent in U.S. dollars. They then loaned up to 95 percent of the value of the deposit back to the depositor as long as the loan amount was reinvested in further FCNR (B) deposits. Because banks were able to swap these funds at 3.5 percent they were able to lend U.S. dollars at 3.7 percent to depositors. Depositors therefore earned 4.7 percent on their 5 percent margin and an additional 1 percent on 19 times their money from the spread on the leverage offered to them. Therefore, they were able to earn a fixed three-year return of 23.7 percent per year on their deposits. This obviously became very popular with NRIs, and by November 2013 banks had raised almost $25 billion in FCNR (B) deposits. Obviously, as banks exhausted their capital and exposure limits, they increased the cost of leverage and the returns to later depositors were lower. The RBI closed the subsidized swap window on November 30, 2013. However, for those depositors who had spare liquidity and were able to board the gravy train during this short window, they got nothing less than a free lunch from the RBI.

EQUITY MARKETS

India has one of the oldest stock exchanges in Asia. The Bombay Stock Exchange was established in 1875. After independence, India established 23 separate stock exchanges, and almost all major cities and towns in India had a stock exchange. The prominent stock exchanges were the Bombay, Calcutta, Delhi, Madras, and Ahmedabad Stock Exchanges. India has had a well-developed investor base, and the largest minority investor in Indian stocks has been the Gujarati community.

The equity markets in India changed significantly after economic liberalization. The Securities Exchange Board of India (SEBI) was created in 1988 and got statutory powers by an act of Parliament in 1992. The SEBI became the regulator for the Indian securities markets and was modeled on the Financial Services Authority of the United Kingdom and the Securities and Exchange Commission of the United States. There was a lot of resistance to the creation of the SEBI, both within the trading community and within government. In its initial years, the SEBI was a toothless tiger with almost no powers. Over time, the powers of the SEBI have been expanded. However, the SEBI has not been able to exercise the same power and vigor over the capital markets that the RBI has been able to exercise over the banking and payments system. Part of the reason for this is that policy-making powers still vest with the government and Parliament. While the SEBI has streamlined regulations related to the capital markets, its ability to enforce regulations has been found wanting. In recent times, the government has given significant additional powers to the SEBI to indict and punish offenders, but it does not have the depth of management and talent with the confidence and experience to use these powers. To its credit, though, the SEBI has done an excellent job of increasing transparency and disclosure of information by issuers of securities as well as market participants.

The creation of the National Stock Exchange (NSE) in 1993 was another milestone in the development of India's equity markets. The NSE was a 100 percent electronic exchange that operated on an order-matching basis without any market makers. Members connected to the NSE through leased lines or through satellites using very small aperture terminal connections. The onset of the SEBI and NSE era combined with the improvement in technology and connectivity led to several improvements in the Indian markets. The National Securities Depository Limited (NSDL) was launched in 1996 and "dematerialization" of shares was introduced. Physical share certificates were sent back to companies, and shareholder accounts were credited with electronic holdings of shares in their respective "demat" accounts. This was the beginning of the end of the era of bad deliveries and failed settlements. As securities holdings moved entirely to electronic form, the system of weekly trade settlements gave way to rolling settlements where transactions needed to be settled daily. Initially, rolling settlements were introduced on a few securities on a T+5 basis. By April 1, 2003, rolling settlements on a T+2 basis were introduced for the entire equity market.

In bygone eras, trade settlement was carried out on a leisurely basis and the market had a generous *badla,* or carry-forward trading system, whereby trade settlements could be carried forward by paying a cost of carry that was determined by funding providers to the settlement system. With the introduction of rolling settlements and the termination of the carry-forward system, liquidity in the Indian markets became severely constrained. Around this time, the stock exchanges introduced derivative contracts on equities that became phenomenally popular in a very short time. Index futures were introduced in 2000 and single-stock futures and options were introduced in 2001.

India today has one of the most developed equity markets in the developing world, if not in the entire world. The Indian stock exchanges routinely rank among the top three exchanges in the world in terms of number of transactions. There has never been a settlement failure in the country's stock exchanges in recent times. The standards of governance and disclosure have consistently improved. Companies are required to report their earnings quarterly and disclose all significant transactions and activities. The surveillance of the market by the exchanges and the SEBI has also improved significantly, and meaningful manipulations are identified relatively quickly.

The latest significant change in the Indian equity markets has been the introduction of high-frequency trading (HFT) and algorithmic trading. The speed of the introduction of HFT has been fast, even by global standards. The SEBI permitted direct market access to the Indian stock exchanges in 2007 and notified regulations in 2008, ushering in the era of HFT and algorithmic trading. In 2007, right after the regulations were introduced, neither the regulator and stock exchanges nor market participants had any clue with respect to server co-locations, latency, and other HFT requirements. Some brokers who were active in the arbitrage market between cash securities and single-stock futures were enthused by the possibility of having computers execute their arbitrage trades instead of them employing an army of "jobbers." Since then, both the NSE and the Bombay Stock Exchange have allowed the co-location of servers on their premises, and there are several vendors who provide Algo-ORS (order routing system) as a fee-based service, leading to rapid growth in high-frequency and algorithmic trading.

MARKET PARTICIPANTS

India has a well-developed ecosystem of participants in its equity markets. Market participants can broadly be classified into domestic institutional investors (DIIs), foreign institutional investors (FIIs), private corporate bodies (PCBs), high-net-worth investors (HNIs), and retail investors.

DIIs in India are primarily mutual funds and insurance companies. While it has been proposed at various times that pension funds should be permitted to invest in the equity markets, the actual on-the-ground movement on this front has been slow. Mutual funds were introduced to Indian investors in 1964 when the Unit Trust of India Act was passed by Parliament. Until 1987, Unit Trust of India (UTI) was the only mutual fund company in India. In the late 1980s, mutual fund schemes were launched by several public-sector banks. The mutual fund industry was opened to private participation in 1993. Since then, the industry has grown rapidly, with about 46 mutual fund companies in existence today.

The Life Insurance Corporation of India (LIC) was created in 1956 by the nationalization and amalgamation of all private insurance companies and societies that existed in India. The general insurance industry was nationalized in 1973, and all existing general insurance companies were consolidated into four government-owned general insurance companies. A fifth new general insurance company was also created in 1973. Until the onset of economic liberalization, the entire insurance industry was under the control of government companies. The LIC was and continues to remain one of the largest DIIs in the equity markets. In 2000, the insurance industry was opened up to the private sector. Today, there are 27 general insurance companies and 24 life insurance companies operating in India. The participation of private insurance companies in the equity markets grew exponentially, with the regulator allowing insurance companies to launch unit-linked insurance products (ULIPs) in 2005, which are similar to mutual funds with an insurance wrapper around them. With the equity markets booming in 2006 and 2007, money flooded into the markets via ULIPs. However, the high and front-loaded fee structures of ULIPs combined with their lock-ins created big investor disillusionment with these products in the aftermath of the market crash in 2008 and 2009.

FIIs have been permitted to invest in the Indian markets since 1992. In the early days, foreign companies or overseas corporate bodies (OCBs) were also allowed to invest in Indian equities. However, with the discovery of gross violations and round tripping of funds from India back into the country through OCBs, the window was shut down. The SEBI has kept the regulations and their implementation fairly stringent for FIIs. Only bona fide funds with beneficiary investors who meet strict compliance criteria are allowed to register and invest through the FII route. Due to stringent regulations around registration of FIIs in India, many foreign investors have chosen a synthetic route to access the Indian markets. Foreign brokers have developed a derivative instrument called a participatory note (P-note) that is issued offshore India. The investor places an order with a broker outside India, and the broker purchases the securities in its name on behalf of the investor. The broker holds the stock in trust for the investor and issues an offshore contract confirming the purchase and custody. The potential to bypass beneficial ownership disclosures in India has made Indian authorities weary of P-notes, and they occasionally rock the boat to keep misuse of the instrument in check. India taxes capital gains at source, and FIIs are subject to capital gains taxes in India. There a few jurisdictions, the most prominent of which is the small island of Mauritius in the Indian Ocean, that have double-taxation avoidance treaties with India, which exempt them from capital gains and dividend taxation in India. More than 70 percent of foreign portfolio flows into India are routed via Mauritius to take advantage of the tax treaty.

HNIs and PCBs are used synonymously, as HNIs often use corporate vehicles for their investments in equities, and most PCBs that have the resources to invest meaningful amounts in equities are owned by one or more HNIs. HNIs have been significant investors in Indian equities and have been especially active in small- and middle-market companies. Businesspeople and entrepreneurs who have expertise or knowledge about particular industries or know about the prospects of their suppliers, customers, or competitors have been large investors in the stocks of those companies. Not only have they done well for themselves, but they have played in important role in the price discovery and value-unlocking process in the markets.

Retail investors in India are no different from retail investors anywhere else in the world. They usually come into the market at or near the top of market cycles and usually sell out of fear, fatigue, and distress at or near the bottom of market cycles. The average retail investor has not done well investing in equities over time in India. During the market boom between 2005 and 2007, retail participation increased dramatically, and brokers expanded their offices and networks rapidly. The market malaise of the past five years has seen a complete exodus of retail investors from the market. This has had a devastating impact on the businesses of brokers, and many of them have drastically cut back on their operations and laid off staff. I can almost guarantee that retail investors will be back again at or near the top of the next market cycle.

BANKRUPTCY AND FORECLOSURE

With every economic down cycle comes the increase in nonperforming loans in the banking system and the increase in defaults and delinquencies. Indian banks, especially the public-sector banks, suffer from too much due process and less substance. Lenders in India have perfected the art of creating onerous documentation for borrowers. They derive comfort from taking as collateral everything owned by the borrower, including his personal guarantee and those of his family members and then some. Yet they are seldom able to enforce collateral and recover their loans in a timely manner when things go bad. In this regard, banks have more power against smaller borrowers and can often compel them to repay their loans under threat of confiscation of their collateral. The bigger risks are the most visible big-ticket borrowers.

The reason banks were seldom able to enforce their collateral security interest in case of default was the existence of "debt recovery tribunals" (DRTs). DRTs are specialized courts set up to deal with recovery of debts from defaulters of loans specifically to banks and financial institutions. The DRTs suffer from the same due process delays and indecision that plagues India's entire judicial system. It is not uncommon for cases for enforcement of collateral and recovery of dues, even where sufficient collateral exists and where the defaulter is a willful defaulter, to take years, if not decades.

Due to the inefficiency of India's court system and the inability of lenders to enforce collateral, private-sector banks and foreign banks embarked on an innovative strategy to lend to borrowers in India. They would never take large exposures on a single borrower and would always lend to borrowers with a public-sector bank in tow. In a sense, the private lenders would take advantage of the lethargy and slow reaction times of public-sector banks and would front-run them. Where the private lenders noticed early signs of delinquencies, they would quickly exit by putting their assets to the public-sector lenders and leave them holding the bag.

India has a very sophisticated and well-developed equity market comparable with the best in the world; however, the debt markets in India remain underdeveloped. The authorities, including the government and the RBI, have wanted the debt market to deepen and develop, and they have tried several reforms to create an enabling environment. Despite the noblest intentions of the authorities, I do not believe that their actions alone will be able to develop the debt markets in India.

Why has the debt market failed to develop in India? Debt markets deal with fixed-income securities that offer defined payoffs to investors over a defined time period. The risks inherent in debt markets are of two kinds— credit risk or default risk and interest rate risk or duration risk.

Interest rate risk arises from changes in the opportunity cost of capital among various market participants between the time a fixed-income security is issued and the time it is completely paid off. This is a risk that originates in the hands of the holder of the security (for the most part). If a country has an efficiently functioning market system, where trades are settled and where the clearing system ensures protection from default by individual market participants, this risk is handled well by the marketplace.

India has a well-functioning government bond or securities market. This is the only part of the debt market that carries no credit risk and carries only interest rate risk. The Indian government routinely runs fiscal deficits in excess of 5 percent, and the shortfall is met through borrowing in the domestic government securities market.

The corporate debt market (even for the highest-rated corporates) has failed to take off. The reason the market has failed to take off has very little to do with the availability of capital or the existence of securities and market instruments. It has more to do with the weakness of the legal system in India; the nonexistence of strong bankruptcy, insolvency, and receivership laws; and the poor enforcement of existing laws.

The corporate debt market deals with credit risk in addition to interest rate risk, and it is in the case of the former that India is found wanting. What is the challenge? Debt by definition is senior to equity. Within debt, there are securities that are structured as senior and others that are residual in nature. When the going is good and all securities are paid off, the returns to each security holder are well understood. What happens when things go bad, and a company or a special-purpose entity is unable to meet all its payment obligations, holds the key to the development of a vibrant debt market.

Indian law and Indian courts do not accord sufficient sanctity to a private debt held by a private (nonbank) entity. The laws in India are enforced to almost exclusively protect the interest of banks that lend to private entities secured against collateral. In fact, until the securitization of collateral (SARFESI—Securitization and Reconstruction of Financial Assets and Enforcement of Security Interest) act was passed in 2002, as discussed earlier, even banks had to struggle through years of litigation before being able to enforce foreclosure on collateral offered against a defaulted loan. With the enactment of SARFESI, lenders secured by collateral (limited only to banks and recognized domestic financial institutions) could enforce their security interest on a defaulted loan without going through the judicial system. Of late, even enforcement of collateral under SARFESI is becoming difficult, as courts have started accepting appeals by borrowers against lenders enforcing their collateral.

The efforts by regulators and expert committees to fix the system at the transaction level, although noble and desirable, will not be sufficient to allow the development of the Indian debt markets. If the Indian government is serious about the development of the country's debt markets, it needs to pass an act like SARFESI for enforcement of security interest on private debts, and it needs to ensure its effective implementation. The government and the judiciary also need to put in place a strong and effective regulation for organized bankruptcy and reorganization of companies defaulting on their debt.

CASE STUDY: The FCCB Debacle

In a developed market like the United States, if a company is unable to meet its debt obligations, it has to file for bankruptcy where all its equity is written down and where its residual assets are either liquidated or reorganized and allocated to different claimants (society, employees, government, and private creditors) in their order of seniority. While the process can be laborious, lengthy, and prone to high accounting and legal fees, it works and follows the rule of law.

This is not the case in markets like India. Let me share an anecdote. While I was in Switzerland a few years ago for a conference, I met with an interesting individual who shared with me his experience about investing in India.

In the frenzy of all things emerging economies in 2006–2007, an interesting market called the foreign currency convertible bond (FCCB) market developed for Indian companies. These were bonds issued in foreign currency by Indian companies and sold offshore with embedded options for conversion to equity at predetermined premiums. In the go-go bull market of the time, investors lapped them up because the three- to five-year options seemed like no-brainers. For issuing companies, the benefit of lower interest rates on current debt with the potential conversion at a premium to equity at a future date seemed too good to pass up. Billions of dollars' worth of FCCBs were issued by several Indian companies and absorbed by foreign investors.

The story became interesting with the financial market collapse of 2008–2009. Stock values plummeted, the embedded options in the FCCBs went deep out of the money, and prices of the bonds themselves lost more than half their value.

This individual I met in Switzerland told me that in July 2009, he purchased about a million U.S. dollars' worth of FCCBs of an Indian company at 60 cents on the dollar. The total issue size was $10 million, and the bonds were due for maturity in June 2010. In his analysis, he found that the company had $50 million of cash and no other meaningful debts to speak of.

During all of 2009, investors in the FCCB market remained in a state of panic. They eagerly negotiated settlements with issuing companies, and many of the bonds were redeemed by companies (or bought back) at 50 to 60 cents on the dollar. This obviously sent signals to the solvent company in which my new acquaintance had invested that they somehow did not need to repay the entire debt outstanding. So when time came to pay up in 2010, this solvent company with a robust equity market capitalization indicated default and chose to enter negotiations with debt holders.

My acquaintance flew to India during this time and threatened legal action on the CEO. The CEO chose not to antagonize him and paid him in full. However, he paid him only 60 cents on the dollar officially (the amount he had negotiated with all the other FCCB holders) and paid him the remaining 40 cents under the table. I was blown away by this story.

The reason the CEO was able to get away with his shenanigans was that the court system in India is slow and inefficient and the law does not sufficiently protect the interests of private creditors. When a company indicated inability to pay and defaulted on its FCCBs, owners of the bonds had the right to file a "winding-up petition" in the courts against the company. However, the process is so weak and can be stalled and delayed by companies so easily that companies can continue to remain in business, their stocks can continue to trade, and their owners can continue to enjoy salaries and dividends while creditors wait for years and sometimes decades for justice to be delivered.

That is why the bondholders agreed to settle with the company and chose to take the 60 cents offered to them in the present than to have their entire capital tied up for years. My acquaintance was the only bondholder to make some noise, and the CEO in his prudence paid him off to avoid the prospect of litigation and the very minor prospect of an unfavorable outcome.

Until the law and its implementation and protection for private creditors, both secured and unsecured, improves in India, the country's debt markets will remain shallow and underdeveloped.

How does the existence of a vibrant debt market benefit the U.S. economy, and how does it harm the Indian economy? The entire Indian economy is dominated by the commercial banking system. The banking industry is dominated by government-owned banks, which, although very well run, are effective oligopolies. India is one of the few places left in the world where banks are able to earn net interest spreads of 3 percent to 4 percent on their loan books and are extremely profitable in their plain vanilla deposit-accepting and loan-making business.

The usury by the Indian banking system exacts a huge toll on Indian companies (borrowers) and significantly reduces the efficiency of the Indian economy. With the exception of the 50 largest corporations in India, which are large enough to be rated externally and borrow in foreign currency internationally, all Indian companies are dependent on the banking system for their debt-financing requirements.

The U.S. debt markets allocate capital very effectively and creditworthy borrowers are able to raise debt resources on very competitive terms. Even noncreditworthy and high-risk borrowers are able to raise resources (albeit at high cost) to enable them to undertake their high risk (in aggregate adding to the vibrancy of the U.S. economy) ventures.

Developed and deep financial markets are therefore a vital asset for an economy. Unless the government in India is able to put in place the structural changes required to its legal and regulatory systems and ensure their effective implementation, its debt (and hence capital) markets will remain underdeveloped, placing its corporations at a disadvantage to those domiciled in economies with developed capital markets.

RISK AND CAPITAL

A very important part of India's financial architecture is the appreciation and understanding of risk, capital, and the expected return on capital in the business community, the government as well as the bureaucracy. In developing economies, one cannot take this understanding for granted, and there are many countries where this concept is not clearly understood.

The concept of a joint stock company where minority capital providers pool their capital together to invest in the management capabilities of entrepreneurs and professional management teams, who in turn employ skilled specialists to provide goods and services to the consumers, was introduced by colonial rulers into India. This concept has been ubiquitously understood, appreciated, embraced, and used by Indians over the past 200 years. Incognito minority equity ownership requires an element of trust and reciprocity. The ethos that one must not cheat one's partners is very strong in India. Still, many entrepreneurs and business owners don't get it.

Capital in India has always been scarce and has always had a cost. Indians therefore intuitively understand and demand a relatively high return on capital. Indians seldom invest for fulfillment of false grandiosity and for appearances. This makes India a paradise for value investors.

To the casual observer it appears strange that there exist so many business "groups" in India that operate in a large number of disparate businesses that have no apparent synergy with each other. The synergy that each disparate business has with the other is that each of them requires capital. As India's growth has accelerated, opportunities have mushroomed in sector after sector, while there has been a shortage of capital to invest in them.

This has made groups that have strong cash flows and that have strong core businesses become the preferred incumbents for new opportunities in every sector. First-time visitors to India will therefore be surprised to encounter wealthy business groups that have "one of each" in all rapidly growing sectors of the economy.

SUMMARY

India has a robust financial architecture that gives investors the possibility of participating in almost every area of the Indian economy. While the building blocks are in place and the intent and direction are right, more work is needed to bring India's financial system completely at par with the developed world.

Investors often complain loudly about events like the FCCB debacle that leave them with a sour taste about India. Such events seldom repeat themselves. Investors and India's financial ecosystem are both self-correcting. They constantly learn from mistakes and improve and upgrade themselves.

The strength of India's financial system is not sufficiently appreciated by investors. It is one of the most important attributes that will help India sustain and grow at high rates for an extended period and that will help investors make above-normal returns by investing in that growth.

CHAPTER 5

Value Investing in India

I have spent the past 15 years investing in the Indian equity markets. I was fortunate to have been mentored by some of the most experienced investors in the Indian markets. While human nature of hope and fear is universal and markets in India behave no differently from markets anywhere else in the world, there are several characteristics that are unique to the Indian markets. I believe that India is a paradise for value investors and is one of the biggest untapped opportunities in the world. But, unfortunately, the market is also infested with value traps. Separating the true values from the value traps is what keeps the game interesting and challenging.

RISK ON, RISK OFF, AND GLOBAL CAPITAL FLOWS

Foreign institutional investors (FIIs) were permitted to invest in India after economic liberalization in 1991 and have since become major participants in the Indian markets. FIIs hold more than 20 percent of India's market capitalization of $1 trillion and invest almost $25 billion a year into the Indian markets. This level of participation makes FIIs the single biggest investor segment in the Indian markets and their actions disproportionately impact the performance of the markets in the short term. While India has attracted investments from a lot of patient and long-term investors like sovereign wealth funds, government retirement plans, pension funds, university endowments, and foundations, the country has also attracted investments from "hot money" investors like exchange-traded funds, leveraged hedge funds, and the like.

The large participation by FIIs in the Indian markets makes them vulnerable to sentiment and flows in the global financial markets. Therefore when markets globally are feeling good and when they are in a "risk-on" mode, India attracts a lot of FII inflows that have a steroidal impact on the Indian markets and causes the currency to appreciate. However, when markets globally are in a state of fear and despondency and when they are in a "risk-off" mode, FII inflows into the country tend to dry up, and occasionally the country also experiences some outflows.

These ebbs and flows make the Indian markets very volatile and make them what is often referred to as a "leveraged beta" play on the global markets and the global economy. They also create a peculiar liquidity situation whereby those stocks that see interest and participation from FIIs tend to see high-quality sell-side brokerage research, have better liquidity, and command higher valuations than those stocks that do not. The situation has been exacerbated by the fact that in the aftermath of the global financial crisis, participation of domestic investors in the Indian markets has plummeted. The series of corruption scandals witnessed in the past few years, followed by the complete seizing up of the government and the policy-making apparatus, has further damaged domestic investor sentiment. Domestic institutional investors (DIIs) like mutual funds and insurance companies have seen net outflows from investors and have been continuous sellers in the markets. High-net-worth investors (HNIs), private corporate bodies (PCBs), and retail investors have also sequentially retrenched from the markets in the past five years. The lack of participation by domestic investors has completely eroded participation in stocks that do not see FII interest. Liquidity there has completely dried up, and valuations have been derated to unrealistically low levels.

This has created a completely divided market in India. On the one side are stocks that are followed, liquid, and command fair to high valuations; on the other side are stocks that are not followed, illiquid, and trade at unrealistically low valuations (if they trade at all). Investors often erroneously assume that the division is along market capitalization and that the larger stocks are followed and liquid and that the smaller stocks are less followed and less liquid. That is, in fact, not the case. While the largest 30 to 50 stocks that are in various indices are indeed followed and liquid, there are several stocks with market capitalizations that exceed $1 billion that are completely illiquid and very poorly covered by sell-side research. There also exists a universe of smaller companies in the $200 million to $500 million market capitalization range that are fancied by FIIs and domestic speculators, are fairly liquid, and trade at premium valuations. Therefore, the divide is between followed and unfollowed stocks rather than between large-cap and small-cap stocks. To that end, the performance of the market averages like the Bombay Stock Exchange (BSE) Sensex and the National Stock Exchange (NSE) Nifty are poor indicators of the performance and health of the overall markets.

The BSE Sensex is composed of the 30 largest stocks, while the NSE Nifty is composed of the 50 largest stocks, with an almost complete overlap between the two. The indices are market capitalization weighted, and the components of the two indices make up more than 70 percent of India's market capitalization. Compared to the U.S. markets, where the Standard & Poor's (S&P) 500 index comprises the largest 500 stocks and makes-up 70 percent of its market capitalization, the capitalization of the Indian market is very skewed at the top end. The Indian market was rerated between 2002 and 2003, when there was a structural shift in global institutional portfolios to include India in their allocations. This led to an increase in the Sensex from 2,800 levels in 2002 to 20,800 levels in 2007. While the entire market rallied between 2002 and 2005, the broader market rally had fizzled out by the end of 2005. Between 2006 and 2007, the Sensex outperformed most stocks in the market, and it also outperformed most investment managers. In 2007, Morgan Stanley published a report that estimated that only 14 stocks in the Sensex had outperformed the Sensex in 2006. The only exception was speculator-driven stocks and overleveraged story stocks like infrastructure and real estate, which outperformed the Sensex. However, between 2008 and 2009, these stocks went on to lose 95 percent of their value.

I've often heard the refrain from investors and analysts that the Indian markets are always more expensive than their peer BRIC (Brazil, Russia, India, and China) countries, and that the Indian markets always trade at premium valuations. The frustration has become greater, as the premium valuations have persisted even as the Indian economy has slowed down and its growth outlook has deteriorated compared to the other BRIC countries. In better times, the Indian markets have traded at an average price-to-earnings (P/E) multiple of between 18 and 22 for the Sensex, and in slower times the markets have traded at an average P/E of between 12 and 14 for the Sensex. Compared to Brazil, Russia, and China, which have at times during the last decade traded at P/E multiples of less than 10, the Indian markets have always appeared expensive. This probably has to do with the fact that the Sensex is made up of some of the largest noncyclical companies in the Indian economy from sectors like consumer goods, pharmaceutical, media, financial, and engineering, which usually command higher valuations. The indices in Brazil, Russia, and China, however, composed predominantly of cyclical and commodities companies that usually command lower valuations. Some names in the Sensex and Nifty that have always commanded premium valuations due to the nature of their business and franchise or due to the quality of their management, governance, and disclosure standards are ITC (ITC: IN), Hindustan Unilever (HUVR: IN), Sun Pharmaceuticals (SUNP: IN), Lupin (LPC: IN), Ranbaxy (RBXY: IN), HDFC (HDFC: IN), HDFC Bank (HDFCB: IN), and Larsen & Toubro (LT: IN). These names trade at premium valuations even in an economic slowdown like now because they have nonreplicable franchises, and the underlying demographic potential of India will make them potential significant winners over time.

LIQUIDITY, VOLATILITY, AND RISK

Ben Graham and Warren Buffett consider risk as the potential for a permanent loss of invested capital. The capital asset pricing model (CAPM) considers risk as the price volatility of a given stock or security. The three attributes that cause these two definitions of risk to overlap are leverage, time-horizon mismatch, and liquidity. In the case of institutional investors, one more attribute that causes them to overlap is investor expectation mismatch. If the fundamentals and underlying business of a company are strong, and if a significant decline in stock prices is caused either by an exogenous environmental factor or by a one-off event in the company, the volatility presents an opportunity to buy.

CASE STUDY: Mahindra & Mahindra

Mahindra & Mahindra (MM: IN) is the largest tractor and farm equipment manufacturer in India. It also has a utility vehicle business that has grown to include a range of passenger cars. M&M is run by Anand Mahindra, and the group has maintained high standards of corporate governance. M&M has incubated several businesses, including a real estate subsidiary Mahindra Lifespaces (MLIFE: IN), which focuses on developing special economic zones; an information technology (IT) services subsidiary, Tech Mahindra (TECHM: IN), which is among the top five IT services companies in India; a holiday and leisure subsidiary, Mahindra Holidays and Resorts (MHRL: IN), which focuses on time-share holidays; a financial services subsidiary, M&M Financial Services (MMFS: IN), which provides financing to buyers of Mahindra's as well as its competitors vehicles; a steel subsidiary, Mahindra Ugine (MUS: IN); and an auto component subsidiary, Mahindra Forgings (MFOL: IN), among many others.

　　Although many of the group's businesses are cyclical and are impacted during recessions, the group has run its businesses well, and they remain resilient during such periods. In December 2007, M&M's stock price touched a high of INR430 (split adjusted) and its market capitalization was $3.5 billion. By December 2008, in the aftermath of the Lehman crisis, the stock had fallen to INR120, leaving the company with a market capitalization of a $1.20 billion. At that valuation, the company traded at less than one time its consolidated book value for that year and only four times its after-tax earnings for that year. One could easily look through to each underlying business and see that the businesses were doing well and were likely to do better in the future. The businesses had not been affected by the crisis, and the volatility in the stock price was an opportunity to buy. The stock remained in the doldrums all the way until March 2009, giving investors plenty of time to research the company and its businesses and to buy the stock. In March 2009, global market sentiments changed, and by October 2009 the stock was back at INR430. The stock has continued to perform well in line with the performance of its underlying business.

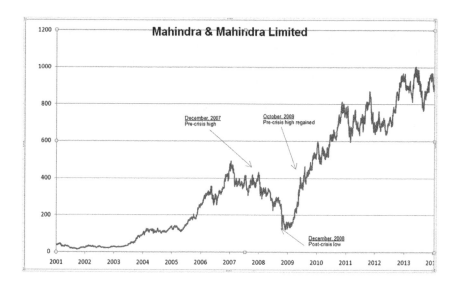

However, if a significant decline in a stock is caused by a fundamental deterioration in the underlying business, then the volatility represents a permanent loss of capital.

CASE STUDY: Unitech

Unitech (UT: IN) is one of the large property developers in India and epitomizes poor corporate governance and misallocation of capital. Companies like Unitech are infamous for their opaque dealings and give the property development sector in India a bad name. The company was a virtual unknown until 2003. By 2004 the market had started to realize that the company had built a large land bank in the National Capital Region (NCR) and the stock caught the fancy of speculators and hot-money investors. The stock went from INR 1.00 (split adjusted) and a market capitalization of $30 million in December 2003 to INR530 and a market capitalization of $15 billion by January 2008. During this journey, the company raised almost $2 billion from the markets at inflated valuations, taking its book value up from $30 million to $2 billion. It also raised debt of almost $2 billion on its balance sheet in line with the equity capital it raised.

Unitech did everything wrong, and by December 2008 its stock had fallen 95 percent to INR30, leaving the company with a market capitalization of $800 million. There were several investors who probably thought that Unitech presented value at those prices and bought the stock. The stock bounced into 2009 and tripled from its depressed levels back to INR100 per share.

Bad companies with bad management always have bad news following them. The company "diworseified" its business into telecom in partnership with Telenor of Norway. Unitech, along with several other companies, allegedly bribed the then telecom minister to allot airwaves on a preferential basis. This broke out as a scandal in 2010, and Unitech's stock price plummeted again; by December 2011 it was down, at INR22. Unitech's stock has continued to decline while its underlying business has gone nowhere and while the bear market has brought out skeleton after skeleton from its closet.

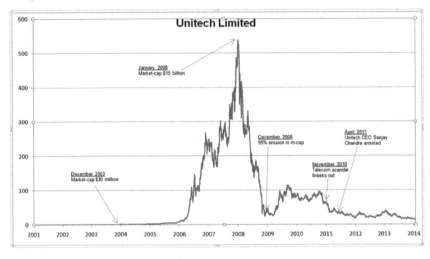

If an investor carries leverage in his or her portfolio, then volatility truly becomes the only definition of risk for the investor. A sudden decline in the price of a stock, whether due to fundamental reasons or other reasons, results in margin calls that force the investor to fold his or her hand prematurely before the underlying thesis has had an opportunity to play out. Similarly, in periods of crisis and when volatility heightens, capital availability (equity and debt) tends to dry up for companies. In such an environment, leveraged companies whose business models require them to continuously raise capital find that their businesses become fundamentally impacted by the external market volatility, and both their businesses and their stock prices deteriorate rapidly.

I have been a frequent visitor to Omaha in recent years to attend the Berkshire Hathaway annual meeting. While it is great to hear Warren Buffett and Charlie Munger speak for six hours about their rich investment and life experiences, the opportunity to meet like-minded people from around the world was for me an equally important reason to attend. In past years, before Wesco Financial was merged into Berkshire Hathaway, Charlie Munger used to host a Wesco investor day in Pasadena on the Tuesday following the Berkshire Hathaway meeting. The format of the Wesco meeting was very different from that of the Berkshire meeting and it mostly consisted of the witty and irreverent Charlie Munger playing "Socratic solitaire" on stage, where he would ask questions and answer them himself, with the audience of about 500 people listening in rapt attention. It was like a pilgrimage for us to head to the West Coast to hear Charlie Munger speak at the Wesco meeting after the Berkshire meeting in Omaha. In one of these meetings, Munger took a dig at the audience and said that over the years he had met many smart people who came to the Berkshire and Wesco meetings to try and figure out what Buffett and Munger did well and to try and do it faster. He said that their strategies primarily involved the use of leverage to speed up the process. Munger said that these otherwise smart people missed the key attribute that made Buffett and Munger successful, and that attribute was time. The two of them were successful because they were in no hurry and they let things take the time that was needed. He reiterated in his own words Buffett's famous statement that you cannot have a baby in one month by getting nine women pregnant.

Time horizon mismatch is another important attribute that can make price volatility risk for an investor. If the investment thesis of a particular stock is likely to take three to five years to play out, an investor needs to have the stomach for volatility in the interim. However, for an investor who benchmarks himself to quarterly or even annual portfolio performance, extreme volatility can disappoint or scare him and make him exit otherwise fundamentally sound companies. This situation gets exacerbated by the volatility of liquidity in markets like India. At times of extreme dislocations, liquidity in the markets in India completely dries up. At these times, it becomes very difficult to sell or exit positions and the impact costs of such actions become very high. Investors who carry time horizon mismatches in their portfolios and get perturbed by excessive volatility often force them to exit positions in very thin and illiquid markets, further exacerbating the volatility in the markets. The circle becomes vicious and almost self-fulfilling, throwing up numerous opportunities for the equanimous and disciplined investor.

In the institutional setting, it is very important for an investment manager to manage a portfolio in line with the expectations of his or her investors. Alternatively, it is important for him to communicate the underlying strategy of the portfolio and the likely outcomes in different market conditions to investors. Where investors are not aligned with the strategy of the portfolio, it is the duty of the investment manager to fire the investor. However, this very rarely happens in the institutional setting, where the pressure to garner assets under management and to increase fund size is very high. As a result, during times of excessive volatility, funds face redemptions from panicked investors, and at exactly the time when they should be adding to their positions, they are forced to sell positions into thin and illiquid markets.

VALUE TRAPS

When it comes to investing in stocks, there are lots of investment "styles" that people follow. I often get asked whether I am a Ben Graham–type value investor or whether I am a Phil Fisher–type growth at a reasonable price (GARP) investor. Am I a bottom-up investor, or am I a top-down investor? Am I a diversified investor, or am I a concentrated investor? As Warren Buffett says, all investing is the same, and one can call all investing value investing. Investing is about laying out capital today with the expectation of getting it back in the future with a return while safeguarding against losing some or all of that capital in the process. Value investing is buying something today for less than what it is intrinsically worth, with the expectation of selling it in the future at a valuation that is near fair value and by definition higher than today.

How one determines what something is worth is the art of investing. There are no benchmarks, and value lies in the eyes of the investor. Some investors might come to the conclusion that the franchise of a consumer goods company trading at 25 times earnings is intrinsically worth significantly more for various reasons and might consider it a value investment, while some others might believe that a net-net trading at 50 percent of the value of cash on its books is a value investment. Most often, however, people associate value investing with buying stocks cheaply and generally believe that value investors do not like paying up for companies that are fast growers.

Buying a value is not sufficient for making a successful investment in the market. The investment becomes successful when the value in a stock unlocks and when its price converges with its intrinsic value. When Ben Graham was asked by Senator Fulbright, during a Senate Banking Committee hearing in 1955, what makes the price of a stock converge with its intrinsic value, Graham said that it was one of those mysteries that he did not have an answer to. But he said that if one is right on the intrinsic value, the stock does go up to trade around it in a reasonable period of time.

Charlie Munger, quoting mathematician Carl Jacobi's maxim, states that to find the solution to a problem one must "invert, always invert." Therefore, instead of asking what makes a value, one must invert and ask what does *not* make a value? Or, instead, one must ask what makes a value trap? Similarly, instead of asking what makes the price of a stock converge with its intrinsic value, one must ask what prevents the price of a stock from converging with its intrinsic value.

Every value investor can relate stories of having bought stocks that appeared cheap only to watch reality catch up, to see the stock correct more than 50 percent, and to then find the stock expensive at the reduced levels.

When investing in markets like India, the distinction between a value and a value trap becomes much harder. While I am not a big believer in the efficient market hypothesis, I do believe that the collective action of millions of participants does make a lot of news and imminent news to get factored into stock prices. It is always hard to forecast or predict news and developments that come out of left field, and even the most experienced investors get caught with those mistakes. Similarly, most value investors will also be able to relate stories of having bought stocks that appeared cheap only to watch them sit around and do nothing for years, causing them fatigue and frustration and eventually forcing them to sell while hopefully at least getting them back their initial capital.

In my experience, especially in markets like India, the two most important attributes that make a stock a value trap instead of a value are poor corporate governance and poor capital allocation. It is the same two attributes that also prevent a stock from converging with its apparent intrinsic value.

I use a simple five-step framework to evaluate stocks in my idea universe and to separate the value traps from the values. It is not a rigid formula or quantitative scoring system; rather, it is a qualitative framework with the five filters or hurdles serving more like guideposts.

Each stock or idea needs to get through one filter before it can move on to the next one. The process is dynamic, and iterative and stocks are constantly evaluated against the filters even once they make it into the portfolio. The five filters are used sequentially in the following order:

1. Corporate governance
2. Capital allocation
3. Business fundamentals
4. Financial strength
5. Relative opportunity

CORPORATE GOVERNANCE

Since the turn of the twenty-first century, corporate governance has been a hotly discussed and debated subject. With the failures of Enron and World-Com during the early part of the previous decade and the failures at Bear Stearns, Lehman Brothers, and AIG during the financial crisis of a few years ago, commentators have lamented the decline in governance standards and the rise of financial frauds in Corporate America. India has had its own set of scandals, with the disappearance of companies like DSQ Software and Pentamedia Graphics during the early part of the previous decade and the collapse of Satyam Computer Services during the financial crisis a few years ago. The most recent governance scandals in India have been those around corruption and leverage in the resources and infrastructure sectors of the country.

When I evaluate stocks for corporate governance, I do not focus on securities law violations and outright frauds. That is a given, and that is a ticket to the dance. I evaluate stocks for adherence to a more subtle type of corporate governance. Most companies in India are owned by a dominant or majority shareholder colloquially called a "promoter." Even in companies where there is no clearly identifiable promoter, management teams tend to be very well entrenched and often have very strong influence over the board. I try to evaluate whether the promoter or the management treats and is likely to continue treating passive minority shareholders like equal partners in the business and whether the company is run keeping in mind and safeguarding the interests of minority shareholders.

Unfortunately, such an evaluation is not binary. It is very subjective and instead of being black and white consists of many shades of gray. It is also not static. As promoters and managements evolve and change, some of them maintain high standards of minority shareholder protection, some maintain poor standards of protection, some improve their standards of protection over time, and some others see their standard of protection degenerate and deteriorate over time. How does one identify poor corporate governance, and when is a particular violation condonable and another not condonable? In the famous words of Justice Potter Stewart of the United States Supreme Court when asked how he defined pornography, "It is hard to define it but I know it when I see it."

Identifying poor corporate governance is an exercise in subjectivity, and no two investors will agree on what is forgivable and what is not. If one sets the bar of corporate governance unrealistically high, then one will never buy a stock. Some examples can probably better illustrate the challenge.

In 2002, Anil Agarwal controlled Sterlite Industries (STLT: IN), which, by approval of the Bombay High Court and the Registrar of Companies, initiated a buyback scheme whereby it mailed checks of INR100 in cash and INR50 in the form of bonds to minority shareholders offering to buy back their shares for a total consideration of INR150. What was unique about this scheme was that all shareholders were considered willing sellers unless they decided to opt out by sending a signed form back to the company. The book value of the company at that time was INR300, but the market price of the company was 105. Minority shareholders and the Securities Exchange Board of India (SEBI) cried foul at the scheme, but the Bombay High Court upheld it, giving a three-month extension period to minority shareholders to respond in case they wished to opt out. The holding of the promoters went up from 43 percent to 67 percent. The promoters' contention was that, although innovative, the scheme was completely fair because investors had a full right to opt out and the offer was at a 40 percent premium to the then market price. Minority investors contended that many investors did not have the ability to understand the significance of the transaction and probably mistook the money received for dividends. In 2003, Sterlite Industries' holding company changed its name to Vedanta and listed on the London Stock Exchange at a premium. Was this a violation of corporate governance or not? Should one pass Sterlite Industries and its group of companies through the filter of corporate governance and let it go to the next filter, or should it be rejected at this filter itself?

In 2007, Mahindra & Mahindra (MM: IN) acquired a 43 percent stake in competitor Punjab Tractors for a price of INR360 per share. Punjab Tractors helped M&M increase its market share in the Indian tractor market from 31 percent to 40 percent and helped it dominate the North Indian market. The company made a tender offer for 20 percent additional shares to the public at INR360 as per SEBI regulations and was able to acquire the shares, taking its holding in the company up to 63 percent. Over the next year and a half, M&M cleaned up Punjab Tractors' operations and made it a much better run company than when it had acquired it. In August 2008, M&M approved a merger of Punjab Tractors into the company, offering minority shareholders of Punjab Tractors one share of M&M in exchange for three shares of Punjab Tractors. In the aftermath of Bear Stearns' implosion in March 2008, the Indian markets had corrected meaningfully. Shares of M&M were trading at INR580, down from INR860 at their peak in December 2007. Shares of Punjab Tractors were trading at INR220 prior to the merger announcement. M&M's contention was that the intrinsic worth of M&M was substantially higher than its quoted market price and that the valuation of the two companies had been done by independent valuers. It also contended that the INR360 price paid for acquisition in March 2007 included a substantial control premium. Minority shareholders of Punjab Tractors contended that the share swap offer made by M&M valued the company at even less than its already depressed share price of INR220. They also contended that at no point in its history had M&M traded at a price higher than INR900. At that price, a share swap ratio of 3-to-1 valued Punjab Tractors at less than the INR360 M&M had paid for a much worse company only 18 months earlier. Was this a violation of corporate governance or not? Should one pass M&M and its group of companies through the filter of corporate governance and let it go to the next filter, or should it be rejected at this filter itself?

Novartis India (HCBA: IN) is a 75 percent–owned subsidiary of Novartis AG of Switzerland. It was one of the many popular and loved listed multinational corporation (MNC) subsidiaries in India, although over time the market has fallen out of love with Novartis India. Novartis AG itself has fallen out of love with India. It has had a lot of bitter experiences with India. First, it was forced to list its subsidiary on the stock markets; then, when the law changed, permitting it to delist, it was unable to delist because of what all MNCs claim are overly favorable rules for minority shareholders; finally, it has had bitter experiences with intellectual property protection on its patented medicines. Over time, Novartis has incorporated three 100 percent–owned subsidiaries in India. No significant new therapy platforms are being launched under the listed company. In fact, Novartis India has loaned in excess of $130 million of surplus cash to its 100 per-cent–owned subsidiaries, helping them grow their businesses at the expense of Novartis India. Novartis contends that the funds were sitting idle in Novartis India and that the 100 percent–owned subsidiaries pay interest for the money borrowed from Novartis India. It also contends that its global product portfolio and intellectual property is exclusively its own and it does not have any contract or agreement to launch these products through the listed Novartis India. Minority shareholders contend that if Novartis India does not need the cash, it should be returned to shareholders rather than fund the business of Novartis's other companies. They also contend that when they purchased the stock of Novartis India, it was an unwritten con-tract that Novartis India would be the vehicle for all of Novartis's opera-tions in India. Was this a violation of corporate governance or not? Should one pass Novartis India through the filter of corporate governance and let it go to the next filter, or should it be rejected at this filter itself?

Over time, I've built my own rules of thumb and indicators for which shades of gray are acceptable and which are not. The big takeaway from this discussion is that it is important for an investor to look at the attribute of corporate governance in the context of minority shareholder protection in a stock to distinguish a value trap from a value. The exercise of looking for this attribute helps investors avoid the most egregious violators right away and gives investors excellent insight into the operations of their portfolio companies.

CAPITAL ALLOCATION

Most companies destroy the earnings that they retain back with them over time. In fact, Warren Buffett's litmus test for companies is whether they can generate one dollar of market value for every dollar of retained earnings. If they cannot, he prefers that the company return back all its earnings to share-holders. Since most companies are unable to generate returns on retained earnings, Berkshire Hathaway requires most of its subsidiaries to return a substantial part of their earnings back to Berkshire so that it can redeploy the capital in subsidiaries that can make good use of it or so that it can use the capital to acquire more companies. The challenge with Warren Buffett's prescription is that it is antithetical to the tendencies of most managements and company owners. Nobody likes to run a smaller company. Since most companies cannot successfully reinvest capital, Buffett's prescription would require them to keep returning capital to shareholders (like Exxon does). This would make shareholders happy but would not make the company "grow" over time, and at times might even make the company "degrow." What makes shareholders happy does not necessarily serve the interests of management. If that were not the case, no rationale could explain Apple's (and Steve Jobs's) desire to hold $150 billion in cash on its books.

Indian entrepreneurs have historically operated in an environment of relatively scarce capital and have been very focused on generating high returns on equity. When it comes to listed companies, however, we tend to see numerous kinds of peculiarities among promoters in India. The common underlying theme across all these peculiarities is that they destroy returns on equity and are antithetical to the interests of minority shareholders.

A common variety of capital misallocation seen among companies in India is the desire to build "empires." After achieving a particular size or social standing, promoters no longer care about maximizing returns on capital or growing real wealth. Instead, they get carried away by the power trip that accompanies setting up factories and offices across the country and around the world. They expand their businesses for the sake of growth, often taking on a significant amount of debt in the process and risking the long-term well-being of the company and its shareholders (including themselves). They participate in competitive bids to acquire companies in India and overseas and often destroy value in the process.

CASE STUDY: Himatsingka Seide

A company like Himatsingka Seide (HSS: IN) showcases the opportunities as well as the challenges that the equity markets in India present for investors. Himatsingka Seide was founded by Dinesh Himatsingka in 1985, and the company went public in 1986. Himatsingka is a manufacturer of textiles, and until 2005, it occupied a dominant position in the niche space of silk home-furnishing exports from India. The company's market capitalization in 2002 was $30 million, and its book value was $40 million (all figures based on current exchange rates). The company's revenues during the previous five years had grown very incrementally to $25 million, but the company had high margins and consistently earned $7 million to $8 million in after-tax earnings. The return on equity of the company had remained above 20 percent for a long period. The company generated more cash from operations than its net earnings and accumulated cash at a rapid clip. Out of its book value of

$40 million in 2002, the company had $20 million cash on its books. The company had a double-digit dividend yield but had almost no opportunities to redeploy capital at the high rates of return it was earning and kept adding to its cash pile.

The transparency, disclosure, and minority shareholder friendliness that Himatsingka followed despite its tiny size was truly a feather in the cap of Indian entrepreneurs like Dinesh Himatsingka. When I explain to people who are interested in India that there is a large universe of companies in India that "get it," I have companies like Himatsingka Seide in mind. As the bull market of 2003 got under way, Himatsingka got "discovered" and the market capitalization of the company increased to $180 million by December 2005. This sixfold increase in market capitalization in three years happened even as there was no increase in either the revenue or the profitability of the company. In December 2005, at a pre-money price-to-book value of 4, Himatsingka raised $45 million by issuing fresh equity, doubling its book value in the process.

Obviously, I am writing about the company because the story did not end well, or rather deteriorated from its high pedestal. Although the corporate governance and minority shareholder friendliness of the company was top-notch and remains so today, on the capital allocation front, the company lost the plot. There was a generational transition in the management of the company, and Dinesh Himatsingka's son Shrikant Himatsingka joined the company as executive director in 2003. As previously mentioned, the business built by Dinesh Himatsingka focused on a niche segment of textiles and had almost no scope for growth. The business was a cash machine and served the interests of minority shareholders very well. India, however, was turning a new page in 2003, and armed with his undergraduate degree from the United States, Shrikant wanted to make his own mark in the company. There was nothing much for him to do if the company stayed the course it had been on in the past. So with fresh blood in the management, the company decided to "grow" and decided to become a part of the India story. The company set up retail stores in India to market its silk furnishings, as well as diversified into cotton home textiles. Cotton home textiles was and is a commodity business and enjoyed nowhere near the profitability or the returns of the silk textiles business. However, it was a much larger segment and offered large opportunities for "growth." In order to distinguish itself from the other commodity cotton textile producers, the company acquired brands and distributors in the United States and Europe to be able to capture more value from the supply chain. In the process, the company used up all its cash reserves, raised fresh equity, and levered up its balance sheet.

Eight years later, the company's revenues have increased 10-fold from when its empire building started in 2005, and the company struggles to break even on earnings. The company's book value at $100 million is almost exactly where it was after it did the capital raise in 2005, and the company carries debt of $110 million with a big interest-servicing burden. The stock, in the meantime, no longer trades at heady multiples to book value and currently trades at 0.7 times price-to-book value with a market capitalization of $70 million.

The company did nothing wrong or illegal, and I don't blame Shrikant or Dinesh Himatsingka for what they did. They probably did what was in their best interests. However, their interests became misaligned with those of minority shareholders. As a minority investor in a market like India, it behooves one to look carefully at capital allocation and at changes in the motivations and desires of the people behind companies.

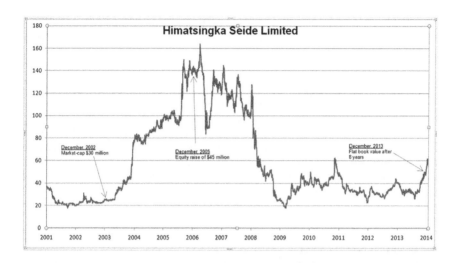

Most companies in India are owned and managed by "families," and the compulsions and motivations of the promoter families are not necessarily aligned with those of minority shareholders. India has no estate taxes. In the joint family system discussed earlier in the book, the wealth of the family can be shared by all members of the joint family without any adverse tax consequences. Let's say a family owns 50 percent of a company and the market capitalization of the company over time grows to $200 million. The net worth of the family becomes $100 million—a lot of money anywhere in the world, but in India, it is an especially large amount. At this stage, one finds that the motivations of the family change from wanting to grow their net worth to dealing with family compulsions like keeping everyone gainfully employed and so on. Sometimes one finds that the entrepreneur or patriarch behind the business becomes contented with achievements thus far and starts to shift focus to spiritual and societal activities. There is nothing wrong with any of these if the owners step back from the operations of the company and let professional management run the show. Unfortunately, the above often happens even while the family keeps the operational reins of the business.

In many companies, one finds that the promoters of the company treat it like their personal property and like their personal piggy bank, even when they own only 40 percent or 50 percent of the company. If the company has a lot of cash or properties, the promoters seriously believe that all of the cash and properties actually belong to them. To them, the minority shareholder is an irritant and does not have a claim on the assets of the company. There are numerous Ben Graham–style net-nets in India, where companies are sitting on large amounts of cash earning next to nothing but where promoters refuse to share anything with minority shareholders and destroy capital and value over time.

CASE STUDY: Bajaj Holdings

Indian market participants and commentators are a biased lot. They often place certain individuals, companies, and groups on a high pedestal, while many others get absolutely no benefit of the doubt. It is important for investors to cut through market opinions in India and to make judgments of their own with respect to corporate governance and capital allocation. One group that is put on a high pedestal by market participants in India is the Bajaj Group. Almost all companies within the Rahul Bajaj faction of groups are admired, and its holding company, Bajaj Holdings (BJHI: IN), is a favorite of the Indian value-investing crowd.

I find the Bajaj Group faltering on corporate governance and Bajaj Holdings miserably failing on capital allocation. Bajaj Auto (BJAUT: IN), the flagship company of the group, is one of the largest two-wheeler manufacturers in India and has created a lot of value over decades. Over time, the company accumulated large cash holdings and incubated a financial services business that became large fairly quickly. In 2007, the company decided to restructure itself by separating the two-wheeler business from the financial services business. The idea to separate the businesses was good; however, the manner in which the company decided to split up the company was completely misaligned with the interests of minority shareholders. The company decided to split itself up into three instead of two companies. Bajaj Auto retained the two-wheeler business, while Bajaj Finserv (BJFIN: IN) was created to own the financial services business. A third company, Bajaj Holdings, was created to hold the cash and investments of the company. But, strangely, the company decided not to do a clean split and instead put 30 percent of the holdings of both Bajaj Auto and Bajaj Finserv into the newly created Bajaj Holdings. Not only did the company not distribute the excess cash to shareholders, it created a convoluted structure to safeguard the interests of the promoter family at the expense of minority shareholders.

By not distributing cash to shareholders during the restructuring, the company clearly communicated that the cash belonged to the promoters entirely and that the minority shareholders had no claim on it. Even though the promoters had done a very poor job of reinvesting cash in the past (unlike Warren Buffett), they maintained that they needed the cash to be able to invest in future businesses. The convoluted structure ensured that the promoters maintained control of all businesses, despite having a less than majority beneficial ownership in all businesses. Digging deeper and looking at family motivations revealed that another reason for the convoluted structure was the group patriarch, Rahul Bajaj's, desire to keep his sons, Rajiv, who managed the two-wheelers business, and Sanjiv, who managed the financial services business, together and his desire to maintain a modicum of control on them. The creation of Bajaj Holdings and the manner in which it was done was completely detrimental to the interests of minority shareholders.

The financial markets and investors have short memories. Investors quickly put the questions surrounding the restructuring of the group behind them and started looking at

Bajaj Holdings as a classic Ben Graham net-net. The market capitalization of Bajaj Holdings is $1.6 billion. It has no debt and has cash and marketable securities worth approximately $500 million. Its holdings in Bajaj Auto are worth $3 billion, and its holdings in Bajaj Finserv are worth $750 million at current market prices. Even if one were to apply a holding company discount of 30 percent to its holdings in Bajaj Auto and Bajaj Finserv, the sum of the parts value of the company adds up to $3.1 billion. Therefore, investors conclude that the company is trading at a discount of 50 percent to intrinsic value and that it is an attractive Ben Graham–type net-net.

Before I proceed further, I submit that in a bull market the stock will probably do well, and it will probably even trade at a premium to book value by some convoluted logic. My goal is to find companies that will do well even in the absence of bull markets. In my opinion, the company is a value trap. The promoters have a very long and poor track record of investing their cash in marketable securities. Minority investors would be much better off if the company used its cash to buy back its own stock, given that it trades at a big discount to underlying value. But buying back stock would be identical to returning cash to minority shareholders. This is unlikely to happen. The promoters' actions at the time of the restructuring clearly established that they believe that all the cash belongs to them and that minority shareholders have no claim on it. Not only do the promoters not let the company buy back stock or declare dividends; they use the SEBI's much-abused legislation of preferential allotments to allot themselves more shares in the company at current discounted values. Neither does the company need the cash, nor do the prices of the allotments reflect the underlying value of the company. While there is no violation of law, the company completely violates the spirit of corporate governance.

Another variety of capital misallocation is where the promoter has a flamboyant lifestyle and "invests" the company's resources in things like jets, sports teams, airlines, or Formula 1 racetracks, or where he has a desire to climb the social ladder and sponsors things like movie awards and swimsuit calendars in the name of promoting the company's brand. These types of "investments" generate poor returns and result in large-scale destruction of capital.

There is another variety of capital misallocation that is harder to identify, where the promoter starts to "diworseify" the company's business. The reason this is tricky to identify is that one has to judge the intent of the action more than the action itself or its outcome. Many promoters have successfully diversified their companies into lateral and sometimes unrelated areas and have done phenomenally well over time, generating high returns on capital. As an investor, one should invest with promoters who have demonstrated such capabilities repeatedly. However, there is a large universe of companies where promoters diversify for the sake of diversification or for external compulsions like providing gainful employment to an offspring. These promoters seldom think about the consequences of the diversification on the return profile and return outlook of the company.

CASE STUDY: EID Parry

EID Parry (EID: IN) is a sugar manufacturer based in southern India and is a part of the Murugappa Group. The company owns 62 percent of fertilizer manufacturer Coromandel International (CRIN: IN). The Murugappas and EID Parry are among those groups and companies in India that have seen an improvement in corporate governance and minority shareholder friendliness over the years. During the 1980s and 1990s, companies in the group had convoluted cross-holdings and often indulged in related-party transactions. The formation of the Murugappa Corporate Board in the late 1990s separated the ownership of the group's companies from its management. All the cross-holdings in the group were unwound, and the promoters engaged with group companies on an arm's-length basis, putting themselves in the same boat as minority shareholders.

Despite being in cyclical businesses, the Murugappas have an excellent track record of capital allocation and value creation. Even though EID Parry is primarily a sugar manufacturer, its founders had incubated businesses in fertilizers, confectionery, and ceramic bathroom fittings. The company has opportunistically invested its capital over the years to create value for its promoters and shareholders. The company had grown its fertilizer business over the decades; consequently, it was appointed as the sales agent for products of Coromandel Fertilizers, owned by Chevron Corporation and International Minerals and Chemicals Corporation. In the early 1990s, when Chevron and IMC wanted to exit Coromandel Fertilizers, EID Parry bought them out. It subsequently transferred its own fertilizer business to Coromandel Fertilizers, streamlining the operations of both companies. Coromandel Fertilizers subsequently acquired Godavari Fertilizers from the government of India and went on to acquire other private companies like Ficom Organics and Sabero Organics. The company later changed its name to Coromandel International. The company today is a powerhouse in the Indian fertilizer industry, with a market capitalization of $1 billion. EID Parry's 62 percent stake in Coromandel International is worth $620 million, which is greater than its own market capitalization of $400 million.

Being a manufacturer of sugar, the company also produced downstream products like sugar confectionery. Over the years, the company expanded its sugar production capacities and transferred the confectionery business into a subsidiary, Parry's Confectionery. The company realized that there was very little synergy between a commodity manufacturing business like sugar and a consumer-facing business like confectionery. In 2004, the company sold the confectionery business to Lotte of South Korea.

The company also grew its ceramics division under the brand name Parryware. With the growth in the Indian economy and the corresponding growth in home building, Parryware did well in the 2000s. Recognizing that the preferences of Indian consumers were changing rapidly, EID Parry brought in Roca Sanitario of Spain as a joint venture partner in 2006. In 2008, EID Parry sold its remaining stake in Parryware to Roca. EID Parry received a total consideration of $200 million from Roca over two stages for the sale of Parryware. The company used the capital realized from the sale to reinvest in and grow its core sugar business. The company has developed a 250-acre food-processing zone on the east coast of India. It has also invested in a 1 million tonne per year sugar refinery in the same zone. The company has incubated a nutraceuticals business that caters to the fast-growing food supplements industry in the United States. It has also incubated a biopesticides business that is used in the cultivation of organic food.

EID Parry has an excellent track record of large value creation using small asymmetric investments, and the promoters of the company are among the best capital allocators in India.

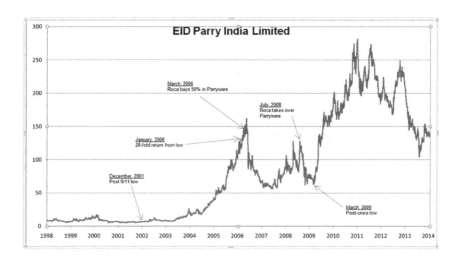

Charlie Munger has said that the most important work is the work on your desk. Quoting Thomas Carlyle, Munger states that "our grand business is not to see what lies dimly at a distance, but to do what lies clearly at hand." Munger's advice is very valuable both in life and in identifying great value investments. The biggest returns are generated by companies that compound capital at a high rate and focus on the mundane tasks that lie before them every day. They follow the philosophy of incrementalism and become incrementally better every day. They don't take big risks; instead, they make incremental capital allocations to small- and medium-ticket investments that generate rates of returns equal to or greater than their existing rates of return on capital.

BUSINESS FUNDAMENTALS

Once a stock gets through the filters of corporate governance and capital allocation, one must look at the fundamentals of its underlying business. It goes without saying that as a value investor, one must look for good businesses trading at great prices. Separating the good business from the not-so-good business is again a subjective process and is once again more art than science.

The U.S. market used to be a value investor's paradise from the 1930s through the 1950s. Sustained economic growth and wealth creation after the war made stocks expensive, and going into the 1960s it became very difficult to find Ben Graham–type "cheap" stocks. The stocks that remained cheap were all cheap for significant reasons. Markets in the 1960s were not cheap like they had been in earlier years. Although expensive in conventional terms, the market did not distinguish between companies that had sustained earning power and those that did not. Warren Buffett, nudged in the direction of Phil Fisher by Charlie Munger, discovered companies that made consumer goods and had strong brands and franchises. These stocks were then still trading at fair prices and offered value to the discerning investor. Of course, toward the end of the 1960s, the markets took the franchise idea to an extreme and came up with the "one-decision" Nifty Fifty stocks, taking them to ridiculously overpriced levels.

Charlie Munger has said that it is better to buy a good business at a fair price than to buy a fair business at a good price. Warren Buffett has said that time is the friend of the good business and the enemy of the mediocre business. Armed with these lessons from the investment greats, investors have approached the Indian markets looking for businesses with strong franchises and moats and avoiding businesses that have any element of cyclicality in them. This has driven prices of consumer goods, pharmaceutical, and multinational companies in India to ridiculously high levels and has kept the valuations of cyclical companies low. The trend has been further reinforced by the global hunt for consumer demand and the promise of India's demographics.

In my experience, in emerging markets like India, where more than 80 percent of the economy is composed of basic goods and services, and where consumer preferences and purchasing power are undergoing dramatic changes over short periods of time, the moats of conventional franchise businesses are not as strong as in mature economies, and the moats of many cyclical businesses are not as weak as in mature economies. For example, in the consumer goods space, the Indian market is completely open to competition, and brands from every part of the world are competing for a piece of the Indian consumer. As a result, consumer brands have very little pricing power, despite ever-increasing production and distribution costs due to entrenched inflation. The costs of reaching the consumer are also continuously increasing due to the proliferation and fragmentation of offline and online media. However, India's infrastructure deficit and idiosyncratic challenges ensure that the economy does not provide a level playing field to all businesses. Many companies in cyclical businesses have entrenched advantages of costs, location, or reach and are able to consistently earn superior rates of return on their capital and are able to outrun their competition. Management also plays a significant role in companies in India and managements of several cyclical companies possess special capabilities and have built entrenched processes that give them significant advantages over their competition.

It is therefore important for investors to evaluate companies on a case-by-case basis and to look at their individual strengths and weaknesses while evaluating whether they have superior or mediocre businesses, and it is important not to get strait-jacketed by conventional thinking on franchises and moats.

CASE STUDY: Godrej Properties versus Godrej Consumer Products

When evaluating the fundamentals of a business, it is prudent to look at the competitive strengths and moats of the business as well as to look at the competitive threats and challenges it faces. The stronger the moats of business, the more sustainable its earning power is likely to be and the higher the valuations it is likely to command. Investors conventionally believe that companies with entrenched consumer brands have strong moats and pricing power because consumer habits change very slowly. However, they believe that businesses like property development are cyclical and possess very few moats. Conventional thinking does not always work in a market like India. In India, moats that appear strong may be weaker in reality, and those that appear weak may actually be much stronger in reality.

The Godrej Group is one of the oldest business groups in India. It is a very well-run group and maintains among the highest standards of corporate governance and minority shareholder friendliness in the country. Godrej Consumer Products (GCPL: IN) is the flagship company of the group and is an entrenched player in consumer goods segments like soaps, hair colorants, toiletries, and liquid detergents. It is one of the oldest and most recognized brands in India, and the company estimates that over 500 million Indians use at least one of their products every day. The business uses virtually no capital and generates returns on equity in excess of 25 percent. The stock of the company trades at a price-to-book value of 9 times. Godrej Properties (GPL: IN) is a property development company owned by the group. The company has development projects in Tier 1 and major Tier 2 cities in India. The company reports poor earnings, generating returns on equity of 10 percent. The stock of the company trades at a price-to-book value of 2.20 times.

Although the consumer products business has a strong franchise, the fast-growing Indian economy and rapidly changing consumer preferences are attracting a plethora of brands into India. Brands from all over Asia, Europe, and North America are pursuing the Indian consumer, fragmenting market shares and destroying pricing power in the process. Due to the fragmentation of media, with a mushrooming of television channels, newspapers, magazines, and online media, the cost of reaching the Indian consumer is also increasing dramatically. In such a scenario, GCPL is finding it hard to grow and hard to protect its margins. This, combined with the fact that the stock trades at a premium that prices-in several years of spectacular growth, probably indicates that the best days of the company as well as the stock are behind it.

Godrej Properties is the real beneficiary of the franchise and brand built by Godrej in India over the past century. The company follows an asset-light model that involves joint development agreements with landowners, and it does not indulge in land banking like its peers in the property development business in India. Housing demand in India is on a secular uptrend. Property development is a location-dependent business and has natural barriers to entry. Most developable parcels of land in Indian cities are already owned and richly priced to reflect that potential. Developers can either buy these richly priced parcels of land for cash or they can enter into joint development agreements with landowners where the developer does not put down capital up front but instead shares the economics from the sale of completed apartments with the landowner in a predetermined ratio. Buying land for cash dramatically lowers the return on capital for property developers. Joint development agreements generate high returns because they involve smaller capital commitments. In joint developments, the landowner takes a big risk of potential nonperformance on the part of the developer. This is where the strength of the Godrej brand comes into play. Landowners are more comfortable entering into joint development agreements with an old and trusted group like Godrej than with a fancy new developer with an insufficient track record. In India, apartments are typically sold by developers while projects are still under construction. In such purchases, buyers take the risk of nonperformance and delays by developers. Recent experiences of serial nonperformance by developers have made buyers even more sensitive to the reputation and the ability of the developer to deliver the promised product on time. Here again, the trust and faith reposed by potential buyers in the Godrej brand goes a long way in alleviating their concerns and worries. As a result of the strong equity of the Godrej brand, Godrej Properties has been able to and continues to expand its business rapidly. The business is likely to grow from strength to strength, making it the dominant company in the group and the returns from the business will likely accelerate as more of its projects come on stream.

FINANCIAL STRENGTH

The fourth filter evaluates a stock for its financial strength. Note that it evaluates it for financial strength and not for financial valuation. In my experience in the Indian markets, companies that generate high returns on equity with little or no debt and generate cash from operations in excess of earnings consistently do very well over time. I have a preference for companies that are cash-generating machines and those that pay taxes. Companies that grow rapidly but that continuously need external sources of funding or those that require increasing amounts of working capital and generate less cash from operations than their reported earnings often have aggressive promoters and managements and often overstate the underlying realities of their businesses. Such companies face significant challenges in times of financial and economic stress.

A high-cash-generating business run by a scrupulous management that is prudent in its capital allocation makes for a stock that is likely to be a winner. When such a stock is available at an attractive price, it makes for the ultimate value investment.

RELATIVE OPPORTUNITY

It is important to diversify one's portfolio, but overdiversification can lead to average returns and is representative of a lack of confidence in one's portfolio and a lack of conviction in one's research and ideas. This last filter deals with the constant evaluation of potential stock investment ideas relative to each other and relative to those stocks already in one's portfolio.

When one compares potential stock investments with each other, one important factor to keep in mind is the asymmetry of potential outcomes.

The larger the asymmetry, the better the potential stock investment. Asymmetry refers to the condition where, in the event of an unfavorable outcome, the stock is cheap enough that it does not fall much, and in the event of a favorable outcome, the stock goes up significantly. In the words of value investor Mohnish Pabrai, asymmetry refers to the condition where if a stock investment is compared to the toss of a coin, then if the outcome is "heads one wins, and if it is tails one does not lose much."

Once one identifies the asymmetry in a potential stock investment, one needs to look at what event or catalyst will lead to a favorable outcome and to the unlocking of value. In my experience, the continuous compounding of capital by companies is the ultimate catalyst that forces the unlocking of value in their stocks. When one purchases a dollar bill at a discount of 50 percent, the value of that dollar bill remains static and unchanged. If another investor buys the dollar bill from one at the end of 3 years, then one earns a 25 percent compounded rate of return on that investment; however, if another investor buys the dollar bill from one at the end of 10 years, then one earns a compounded return of a little over 7 percent on that investment. The outcome of one's investment then becomes a function of time, and time becomes the enemy.

However, if one buys a stock at a discount of 50 percent to book value, and the company compounds its book value at 25 percent a year consistently, then at the end of three years, the book value of the company doubles and the stock at one's purchase price reflects only 25 percent of the book value of the company. At the end of six years, the stock at one's purchase price reflects only 12.5 percent of the book value of the company. If the stock does not get derated and trades at the same 50 percent discount to book value that existed at the time of purchase, then the compounding in the book value of the company forces the stock to increase in value by the rate of growth in book value (i.e., 25 percent). If the consistent performance of the company eventually forces the stock to get rerated over time (as often happens), one's return from investing in the stock exceeds the rate of growth in the book value of the company.

CASE STUDY: Gujarat State Fertilizers and Chemicals

Gujarat State Fertilizers and Chemicals (GSFC: IN) is an example of a company that is an efficient operator in its business and follows the philosophy of incrementalism. It consistently compounds its capital and generates returns for shareholders even while the market continues to rate it poorly. The company is a manufacturer of phosphatic fertilizers and chemical intermediates. The company was promoted by the state government of Gujarat, and it owns 38 percent of the company. The company operates with high standards of corporate governance and is minority shareholder friendly. In 2008, there was a controversy surrounding a circular by the Gujarat government advising state-owned PSUs to contribute 30 percent of their before-tax earnings to charitable causes. This was strongly protested by minority shareholders, and the circular was not implemented. Some investors have worried that the threat of something as egregiously minority shareholder unfriendly as that remains a possibility, and others have taken the view that the positive response from the government indicated their concern for the interest of minority shareholders.

The company is a prudent capital allocator and has compounded book value consistently at more than 20 percent a year while paying a 3 percent dividend and carrying insignificant debt on its balance sheet. The fact that the company is run by bureaucrats and operates within a narrow mandate prevents the company from making large capital misallocations. It incrementally invests in high-return-generating projects that continuously strengthen the competitive moats of the company. The company has consistently generated more cash from operations than reported earnings and has built a war chest of cash. The cash will likely be used by the company to fund its next stage of growth, which will involve doubling of capacities. Given that the cash does not earn high rates of return and acts as a drag on return on equity, a high return utilization of the cash will most likely improve the returns on equity of the company.

One does not often hear compounding mentioned as a relevant catalyst in more mature markets. The reason is that in those markets, companies that consistently compound their book values at high rates very quickly start to trade at large multiples of book value. If a company trades at three or four times its book value, even if it compounds its book value at 25 percent, a consistent derating in its stock price can potentially generate mediocre returns for an investor in the medium term. The good news is that given the relative inefficiency and lack of interest in the Indian markets, one is able to find companies that are compounding capital at high rates and are still trading at modest multiples of their book values.

SUMMARY

The Indian markets relative to their counterparts in developed countries are inefficient. The despondency and poor sentiment of recent years has made the Indian markets even more inefficient. One is able to find high-quality companies with good standards of corporate governance, efficient capital allocation, sustainable moats, financial strength, and high rates of compounding available at modest valuations. The Indian markets are therefore truly a value investor's paradise. They represent the largest untapped opportunity in the world, but only for investors who can think independently and who have the courage to follow their convictions.

CHAPTER 6

Looking Back

The past decade has been an interesting period for India. After the initial euphoria that followed economic liberalization in 1991, the Indian economy faced a difficult period of adjustment between 1997 and 2001. By 2002 the economy had hit rock bottom and animal spirits had completely dissipated. In this backdrop, the massive easing of monetary policy implemented by Alan Greenspan at the Federal Reserve, combined with the loose fiscal policy that accompanied the Afghanistan and Iraq wars, ignited a boom in commodities and emerging markets primarily led by China. India caught the emerging-market tailwind and the Indian economy, and Indian markets became among the best-performing economies and markets in the world. Early investors made significant returns. Whether they were able to retain or exit with any of their gains is another question altogether. Hindsight is always 20/20, and it is easy to comment on the actions of investors once the outcomes are known. Still, it is worth looking back at the things that were done right and the mistakes that were made.

REAL ESTATE

Real estate is one of the most capital-intensive asset classes in the world. It is also one of the asset classes that is most highly correlated to economic growth and wealth creation in an economy. Although India experimented with Fabian Socialism for a period of time, India's mixed economic model ensured that private property was protected and distinct from state property. Indians therefore intuitively understand the concept of rent seeking and how land and real estate derives value from the income-generation potential of its end users.

The hierarchy of end use of land based on its income-generation potential in India is agriculture, industrial, commercial (office space), residential, and commercial (retail) in that order. The scarcity of infrastructure has meant that most land in India is not usable for much more than agriculture.

In addition to the scarcity of infrastructure, as discussed earlier in the book, India has a scarcity of capital. The combination of the two ensures that the cost of carry of land that is currently unusable until it becomes usable is very large. Put another way, the difference in value of land that is immediately usable for one of the preceding productive purposes and that which is not immediately usable is very large. The size of India's population, its demographic bulge, and its consistent pace of urbanization since independence has also meant that Indian cities have consistently grown outward, and land has consistently undergone change of use, although the change of use has not always been predictable. As India started growing more rapidly during the past decade, the demand for end use of land exceeded the natural pace of urbanization, and several large urban clusters were created far from existing inhabitation that caused land to undergo dramatic change of use.

This particular aspect of India's land and real estate market has been the source of many great fortunes, as well as the source of many great shenanigans and disappointments. The creation of new urban clusters created large and sudden wealth for their promoters and ignited the imaginations of many real estate entrepreneurs. The problem with investing in land to benefit from its potential change of use is that it requires investors to have a very long time horizon, sometimes as long as 15 or 20 years, it is an illiquid investment, and almost all the returns from the investment are back-ended in the last few years.

Almost all of India's black or unaccounted money has been used to finance the carry mentioned above. The Reserve Bank of India (RBI) strictly prohibits banks from lending against land or lending for the purchase of land to prevent the tangling up of resources from the banking sector in such speculative, long-duration, and illiquid investments. In the early part of the 2000s, the government of India and the RBI relaxed restrictions on foreign investment in Indian real estate. Even then, the RBI prohibited foreign investment in land by ensuring that foreign investors were not permitted to sell undeveloped land. However, foreign investors were permitted to purchase land for development into compliant projects. Despite the best intentions of the government and the RBI, large resources from the banking sector and a disproportionately high percentage of foreign investment went into the purchase of land with the intention of carrying it until it underwent change of use.

During the go-go years of 2006 and 2007, smart real estate entrepreneurs raised capital from the Indian public, from foreign investors, and from the banking system to build large land banks of cheap land. They were able to do so because their pitch to investors was that as operators they possessed special capabilities that enabled them to change the use of land by will and design. They claimed that they were therefore able to reduce the amount of time that land needed to be carried before it underwent change of use. They claimed that the reduction in the duration of carry made the investment in land more liquid because they no longer needed to sell land to other investors and were in a position to sell developed real estate to end users. This pitch was supposed to help them circumvent RBI regulations for bank lending, as well as foreign investment.

The period from 2003 to 2009 was one of very high growth for the Indian economy, and land in Indian urban centers underwent faster change of use. For the incumbents who owned land, the repricing generated high returns. Almost all of the returns of Indian real estate companies during this period came from the change of use of land and its consequent increase in value. However, they camouflaged it in their real estate development activities and spun long yarns about their unique capabilities, power of their brands, Indian housing demand, and so on. Investors everywhere were attracted to these high rates of return, and several real estate private equity funds were set up by smart managers in a relatively short period of time. These funds exceeded their most optimistic fundraising targets and raised billions of dollars. All of this money went into funding "projects" of real estate companies. These projects were nothing more than large-scale speculation on land, with the hope that the land would undergo change of use relatively quickly, large returns would be earned, and therefore no questions would be asked. Unfortunately for these real estate entrepreneurs and real estate private equity funds, the global financial crisis, the outbreak of corruption scandals in India, and the policy paralysis of the Indian government happened in quick succession, completely stalled Indian growth, and completely seized up the change of land use momentum that had gathered pace in earlier years. As a result, these real estate companies became saddled with large illiquid land banks in peripheral areas with no demand for the marginal developments on these land banks. Their cash flows, which were primarily coming from new capital raising, dried up, and their debt became unserviceable. What appeared to be 3- to 5-year development projects became more like the traditional 15-year land carry investments. Real estate private equity funds, which operate with 7- to 10-year time horizons, got stuck in these investments and were not able to get their money out. Limited partners of these funds were disappointed at the poor outcomes from their investments in the promised land. It became one gigantic illiquid mess, disappointing and upsetting everyone in the process.

Real estate in India is an absolutely terrific investment. No developer who has maintained a liquid balance sheet and invested in projects on currently usable land has ever lost money in India. The returns from these capital-intensive projects are good but not spectacular. But when real estate entrepreneurs get carried away by dreams and desires to become billionaires and to make 100× returns on their own limited pools of capital, everyone ends up losing their shirts. Land carry investments that earn high compounded rates of return once the land undergoes change of use are also very attractive investments. However, they are for investors with a different capital base, risk appetite, investment objective, and investment horizon. They are certainly not for foreign investors whose appetite for illiquidity and whose time horizons are completely misaligned with such investments.

One area in real estate that has attracted a lot of interest in recent times is "affordable housing." The theory is that India has a "shortage" of 50 million housing units today. At the same time, there is unsold inventory in projects in almost all cities of India. The theory is that real estate in India is expensive and unaffordable by most Indians. Therefore, if developers would build affordable housing, more Indians would buy them. I think the concept of affordable housing is a complete misnomer and completely misunderstood. All Indians will not be able to afford buying a home where they would want to live today because they would essentially drive up prices on each other and price themselves out. The market works, and although it is dynamic, a kind of equilibrium does exist. The crux of the problem is that India has inadequate infrastructure and therefore insufficient supply of usable land. If the government went on an infrastructure building spree and made land at distances of 60 kilometers and 100 kilometers from city centers usable by people who work in the city (where the income-generation potential is or jobs are), then the average price of land and hence houses would come down. If civic infrastructure improved and more dwellings and more square feet could be built on the same amount of land, the average cost of a house would come down. I do agree, though, that there is an opportunity for developers to lower the average ticket size of a home and to make them more "affordable" by innovating with materials, designs, and costs as well as by right-sizing the dwelling units.

CASE STUDY: The Land Acquisition Act 2013

As discussed earlier, land is a sensitive subject in India. Given that most of the country is fertile and cultivable, most of the accessible land in the country is privately owned and under agricultural cultivation. As India grows and moves up the value chain from agriculture to manufacturing and services, almost every kind of development requires land. Development therefore requires the displacement of existing owners and users. The transfer of ownership and use from the old to the new involves significant social tension. While it happened on the margins, no one gave much importance to it. However, when the change became large scale, it was handled poorly and gave rise to problems that stalled the development process.

India has had to arrive at a consensus on how to handle this change. New developments involve value creation, and a consensus was needed on how much of the value would be captured by those who were displaced and how much of the cost would be borne by those who would create the new development. Those displaced claimed that new developments would not be possible without their land and desired rents that captured all the upside, whereas those involved in the new developments claimed that high costs of land acquisition would make their developments uneconomical and unviable. A social compact needed to be reached that required both parties to cede ground and to share the costs of and the benefits from development that would result in win-win outcomes for all parties involved. The reason this has been especially challenging is that India is in a unique situation incomparable to any other country in the world, and there were no road maps or precedents available to work with.

The Right to Fair Compensation and Transparency in Land Acquisition, Rehabilitation and Resettlement Act 2013 is landmark legislation that seeks to achieve that social compact in India. There have been many critics of the legislation, and its implementation is going to remain a challenge. However, the act goes a long way in defining numerous contentious boundaries that have plagued the development process in India. It also clearly defines what role the state can play in the process of land acquisition and what rules the state as well as private parties have to adhere to in the process of land acquisition, rehabilitation, and resettlement. It defines clear rules for the compensation and the consent of sellers, and it removes ambiguity from the land acquisition process. While some critics have argued that the act will increase the cost of land acquisition in India and will render many projects unviable, others have said that by defining clear compensation rules, the act clears the way for the speedy implementation of projects. I believe that the cost of land acquisition is something that will get built into project costs and is unlikely to be a deal-breaker for development. I also believe that the bigger problem for project developers was the uncertainty and delays surrounding project implementation and the land acquisition act is the game-changer that will give them the needed certainty.

PRIVATE EQUITY

Private equity is by far the most confused asset class in India. The reason is that India does not fit the convention of global private equity at almost any level. One of the most popular strategies of private equity funds globally is investing in buyouts. In a typical buyout, a private or public company is bought in its entirety by a private equity fund. The fund finances the purchase through a combination of debt and equity. It then restructures the capital structure and the balance sheet of the company and streamlines its operations in various ways to improve the efficiency and performance of the company. In a few years, the fund sells the company to another strategic buyer or relists it and earns a return on its investment in the process. The reason buyouts as a strategy do not work in India is that most Indian companies have a dominant shareholder. These dominant shareholders are smart and have high expectations. They are unlikely to ever sell their stake to a private equity fund at anything less than a full valuation or even a premium to full valuation. There is very little left on the table buying a company at those prices. In cases where the dominant shareholder does sell to a fund, the fund has to be weary and keep in mind the old saying, "Be careful what you wish for—you just might get it." The dominant shareholder is usually integrally intertwined with the fabric and ethos of the company and is much more than the key man. At the end of the obligatory two- or three-year commitment period after the sale, when the original promoter leaves the company, the company often starts to fall apart. There are very few companies where the underlying businesses are so mature, operations so process driven, and cash flows so predictable that the departure of the original promoter does not have a meaningful negative impact. If a superhero private equity fund manager did manage to negotiate a fair purchase price and did manage to find a company that would not fall apart, then he would face the next challenge of the virtual impossibility of delisting a company and taking it private in India. If the fund is unable to take the company private, it would be virtually impossible for it to restructure the company in a manner that would be needed with the constant irritant of dissent from public shareholders.

CASE STUDY: Gokaldas Exports

Blackstone's acquisition of a majority stake in Gokaldas Exports (GEXP: IN) in 2007 was heralded as the game changer in Indian private equity and as the start of the buyout revolution in India. Blackstone spent $116 million to buyout a 50 percent stake in Gokaldas Exports from its promoters and a further $49 million on a tender offer to acquire 20 percent from the public spending a total of $165 million for a 70 percent stake in the company. Blackstone's plan was to professionalize the management of the company that employed 40,000 workers and to change it from a family run company into one of Asia's largest apparel outsourcing companies. It also planned to monetize the real estate underlying the company's owned factories in Bangalore by moving them to special economic zones.

The reality that emerged was very different. In hindsight, the promoters of the company sold to Blackstone at the top of the market. Immediately after the sale to Blackstone, the earnings of the company started deteriorating. The company earned $12 million in after-tax earnings (at today's exchange rates) in 2007 when the promoters sold the company. The following year it earned less than $10 million, and in the following years the company started losing money. The promoters resigned from the management of the company three years after the sale on expiration of their management contract. Blackstone's professional managers have been unable to run the business, and the company has sunk into deeper losses, losing $20 million in the most recent year. While the value of the underlying real estate remains intact or has even risen, Blackstone has realized that it is not easy to move or lay off

40,000 employees in India, and the contingent liabilities are large. The market capitalization of Gokaldas has declined to $35 million, resulting in an 85 percent marked-to-market loss for Blackstone.

The other popular private equity strategy globally is growth capital investing. In this type of investing, the fund invests capital into a company, almost always unlisted, with a large external market opportunity and insufficient resources to capture that opportunity fully. The fund gets actively involved with the company and, in addition to capital, provides strategy and networking to the company to achieve its full potential. The fund usually gets its exit by a stock market listing or a sale of the company to a strategic buyer. In India, it is very challenging to do growth capital investing. The reason is that the costs and barriers to going public in India are fairly low, and most companies with strong underlying momentum in their businesses and a need for capital go public relatively early. Once public, if their performance continues, their ability to access capital both from the banking system as well as from the equity markets becomes relatively easy. The role for a private equity fund investing growth capital becomes significantly diminished in a public listed company, and therefore funds tend to avoid investing in listed companies. The universe of large companies that choose to remain unlisted in India is relatively small. Those that do choose to remain unlisted do so either because they have very strong cash flows and very little capital needs or because they do not want to deal with the headache of having external investors in their companies. Both of these reasons make them unsuitable candidates for private equity growth capital investing. The remaining universe of unlisted companies is fairly large. However, almost all of these companies are relatively small. Although many of them don't have a shortage of ambition and desire to become large with the help of external capital, a large number of them do not have the people and processes to scale up and make that leap. The problem for private equity funds today is that it is unviable to run the fund management business with less than $500 million in assets under management. With $500 million in assets under management, a fund needs to be able to invest at least $25 million in a single company. At investment ticket sizes smaller than that, the resources of the fund become stretched preventing them from meaningfully contributing to the strategies of their portfolio companies. Small ticket sizes also do not move the needle in terms of performance for the fund in the event of successful outcomes. The number of companies in India that are unlisted but still have businesses that are large enough to absorb $25 million are very few in number. Other than real estate, most other strategies of private equity globally like investing in distressed assets, structured credit, or mezzanine securities do not work in India due to regulatory challenges.

The private equity story in India started with the investment of $60 million by global private equity player Warburg Pincus into Bharti Enterprises, now called Bharti Airtel (BHARTI: NS) in 1999. Warburg went on to invest a total of $290 million in Bharti over the following two years. The company went public and listed in 2002. Warburg exited its investment in Bharti by 2005, with a total gain of $1.5 billion. The success of Warburg's investment in Bharti led to an explosion of interest in India from the private equity community. Almost all the global majors in private equity set up shop in India, and several new private equity funds were raised by homegrown talented managers.

The success of Warburg Pincus's investment in Bharti was probably most closely replicated by homegrown private equity fund ChrysCapital. ChrysCapital was founded by Ashish Dhawan and his classmate from Harvard Business School, Raj Kondur. ChrysCapital started life as a venture capital fund investing in Indian technology start-ups, but quickly changed its focus and became a growth-investing-focused private equity fund. After some spectacular successes with growth investing in companies like Shriram Transport Finance, Spectramind, and Suzlon, ChrysCapital once again changed its focus and started focusing on large-ticket investments in listed companies through private placements as well as through market purchases.

CASE STUDY: Shriram Transport Finance

Shriram Transport Finance (SHTF: IN) is a phenomenal success story of private equity in India. The story involves the determination and vision of two individuals, the founder of the company, R. Thyagarajan, and the founder of private equity firm ChrysCapital, Ashish Dhawan. Thyagarajan built Shriram Transport from humble beginnings. He focused on the used truck financing sector that was shunned by all banks and organized financial institutions. With no competition and a captive market, Shriram earned large spreads and derisked itself by building a deep understanding of and strong relationships with its customers. Ashish Dhawan recognized the potential of Shriram Transport and its unique management team. He recognized the transformational role that growth private equity capital could play for the company despite the fact that it was listed and had access to the public markets. In 2005, ChrysCapital invested $20 million in Shriram Transport Finance and its affiliates that were subsequently merged into the company. The growth capital brought balance sheet strength as well as visibility to the company and the group. The company continued to perform well and used its newfound visibility to raise further equity and debt in the process, increasing the strength as well as the size of its balance sheet. ChrysCapital exited its investment in the company in 2009 in tranches with a total realization of $250 million. The fund earned a return of almost 12 times its invested capital in a short span of five years.

What made Shriram Transport Finance a success story for ChrysCapital was R. Thyagarajan's unique attitude toward wealth creation for minority shareholder unlike other promoters in India and Ashish Dhawan's willingness to veer off the trodden path to recognize and make a transformational investment in a company and a sector that was considered conventionally risky by the financial markets.

The private equity industry in India in aggregate has destroyed investors' capital. In order to survive and to continue justifying their high management fees, private equity funds in India have drifted into all kinds of investment styles and strategies. Some funds have morphed into activist hedge funds by investing exclusively in public equities, while others have become venture capital funds by trying to create successful greenfield business models with the power of their capital. Many others have drifted into collateralized lending, circumventing regulations in innovative ways. The recent severe slowdown in the Indian economy, the complete drying of liquidity and the absence of exits in the last few years has made life difficult for private equity players in India. As with real estate funds, most private equity funds focused on India were raised in the 2004 to 2007 period and have either already approached or are in the process of approaching their 7- to 10-year end of lives. The result has been the same as that with real estate private equity funds discussed earlier. The portfolios of the funds have become completely illiquid and unexitable. Fund managers have no incentive to do anything because they are unlikely to earn any carry on their investments and probably will not be able to raise new funds for a meaningful period of time. Limited partners have become frustrated with their inability to take their losses, exit their investments, and redeploy their capital in other promising areas. The private equity industry in India is due for a major shakeout and clean-up. The funds that will emerge after the clean-up will be smaller in size, run by managers with lower expense bases and more efficient operations, and will be significantly more focused in their investment approach and investment mandate.

EQUITY MARKETS

The equity markets in India have been a phenomenal wealth creation story over the past few decades. The past 15 years have been especially extraordinary for the Indian markets. For investors in the Indian markets, the outcomes have not always been great. Given the transitioning nature of

India's economy and given the volatility in global financial markets, many new areas of opportunity emerged in the Indian markets over the past 15 years and many promising areas fizzled out and disappeared. In the late 1990s, when the U.S. markets were experiencing a boom in technology stocks and dot-coms, the Indian markets discovered the opportunity in information technology (IT) services outsourcing and India experienced a technology boom of its own. In the aftermath of the Nasdaq crash in 2000 and the terrorist attacks in New York in 2001, the technology sector in India completely collapsed and numerous scams and financial irregularities came to light.

The easy liquidity created by the Federal Reserve and the Afghanistan and Iraq wars in 2002 and 2003 created a tailwind in emerging markets, and India experienced an unprecedented acceleration in its economic growth. This was the period when a large number of the foreign funds with a focus on Indian equities were set up. These funds invested into a bull market of enormous proportions and reported outsized returns to their limited partners on relatively small bases of capital. Given that these were open-ended funds, they attracted investments into their funds that grew their assets under management between 5- and 10-fold in a span of less than 12 months. Many of these funds did not have the ability to manage these large pools of capital, and extensive style drift was observed in their management. During the same time period, the financial services business in India expanded rapidly and mutual funds and insurance companies experienced unprecedented inflows in their equity schemes from Indian investors.

With the acceleration in India's growth, a big capital investment cycle was put into motion, and stocks that invested in mega projects or made large acquisitions with disproportionate leverage became the market darlings. Almost all of the capital raised by foreign and domestic funds during this period went into these capital-intensive businesses. The collapse of Bear Stearns followed by the collapse of Lehman Brothers and the complete seizing up of the global financial markets, brought the momentum in the Indian financial markets to a complete stop. Although the economy continued to grow for a few more years, the financial markets had been debilitated, and investors lost a very large portion of their invested capital.

The past five years in India have seen a complete reversal of whatever happened in the prior years. Most foreign funds have either eroded their investors' capital in the market or experienced redemptions and have been shut down. Indian investors stopped investing in the Indian markets and have continuously withdrawn their investments from equity schemes of mutual funds and insurance companies, destroying their businesses in the process. Narrow sections of the market continue to attract interest from very long term investors focused on India and remain frothy while the rest of the market continues to languish with lack of interest from almost all quarters. Unlike private equity and real estate, the equity markets in India have already seen a consolidation and clean-up and are perhaps better poised than other asset classes to benefit from a recovery in the Indian economy.

FOREIGN DIRECT INVESTMENT

Foreign direct investment (FDI) into India has been one of the success stories of the past two decades and is the one investment story, which has not experienced a negative ending. Large-scale FDI by Hyundai, Samsung, Vodafone, Coca-Cola, McDonald's, Viacom, Holcim, Allianz, and the like have successfully captured market share and have met or exceeded the expectations of their investors. Investors have faced challenges primarily with respect to regulation and consistency of policy. The challenges have been one off, as in the case of the tax dispute between Vodafone and the government of India, and are not representative of systemic problems. India has the potential to attract FDI in large multiples of the $25 billion a year currently being received. FDI in India is being held back neither by a shortage of investable opportunities nor by an absence of potential returns but by a lack of clarity on the policy front and the slow relaxation of the restrictions on FDI placed by the government of India. For example, India has the potential to attract large-scale FDI in retail and insurance if the government opens up the sectors and if it eases the current myriad restrictions that make investments in them unviable.

The Planning Commission of India has estimated that the country needs about $1 trillion of investment in infrastructure over the next five years. The commission has also highlighted that the government does not have the resources to make the needed investments, and most of it will have to come from private sources both domestic and foreign. The complete failure of the public-private partnership model of investment in Indian infrastructure projects discussed earlier has discouraged private capital both domestic and foreign from investing. If policy makers are able to fix some of the not-so-insurmountable problems facing the public-private partnership model, India can attract a lot of FDI into public-private partnership infrastructure projects. The supply shortages plaguing India's economy can be fixed only by putting in motion a strong investment cycle. Given the shortage of private capital domestically, a big portion of the funds needed to put this investment cycle in motion will have to come from FDI.

In my opinion, the next phase of India's economic growth will be led by large-scale FDI in manufacturing, services, and agriculture, in that order. I believe that India has the potential to attract more than $100 billion of FDI a year consistently for a long period of time. The biggest barriers to the growth of FDI into India are policy and regulation related. Strong political leadership that can work with all stakeholders to build consensus on the direction and pace of change and that can address some policy and regulatory challenges will put India's much-needed investment cycle into motion. A strong investment cycle will unleash the momentum of FDI into India.

DEBT MARKETS

The reason the debt markets in India have remained underdeveloped was discussed earlier in the book. Banks and domestic financial institutions are the primary participants in India's debt markets, which are disproportionately composed of government securities. The participation of domestic investors in the Indian debt markets has been lower than potential. The primary mode of investment in fixed income by Indians has been through bank deposits. The emergence of the mutual fund industry has seen retail investors participate indirectly in the government securities market at the long end and the overnight money markets at the short end through debt mutual funds. However, in relation to the size of the market their participation remains insignificant.

Foreign investment in the debt markets until very recently was highly restricted by the RBI. The RBI under Governor Raghuram Rajan has indicated its intention of lowering the restrictions placed on foreigners from participating in India's debt and money markets. Whether this is a prudent move will be known only many years from now; however, the outcome of these relaxations in the medium term is going to be a tighter integration of India into the global currency and money markets. While India has primarily been an equity play, private and public, during the past decade, the integration will create numerous opportunities for investors and money managers in the fixed-income space. We are likely to see the emergence of almost all kinds of popular fixed-income strategies, including directional, arbitrage, distressed, quantitative, high-frequency and algorithmic, and so on.

As discussed earlier, the one area of India's debt markets where foreigners participated, the foreign currency convertible bond (FCCB) market, ended in disaster due to India's poor laws and their limited enforcement. Changes in India's bankruptcy and foreclosure laws with protection for private debts and speedy judicial proceedings will go a long way in developing India's debt markets. It is my expectation that India's debt and money markets will create many interesting opportunities for investors in the coming decade.

ENTREPRENEURS AND BUSINESSPEOPLE

Foreign investors in India have a love-hate relationship with Indian entrepreneurs and businesspeople. While they love the talent, skill, energy, and motivation that Indian entrepreneurs bring to the table, they hate the fact that they are difficult people to negotiate with and do not always operate in a transparent and above-board manner. People from nonconfrontational and nonargumentative cultures like Japan have an especially difficult time dealing with Indian businesspeople because over the years they have come to realize that Indians make every interaction into a contest, and it is impossible to "win" against them.

While there are stereotypes surrounding every culture and there are exceptions everywhere, I submit that in general it is difficult to work with Indian businesspeople. The most successful investors in India have been those who have aligned their outcomes with those of their Indian counterparts rather than those who have taken the opposite side of the table. The big takeaway is that Indian businesspeople are, on average, very astute at creating wealth and value for themselves. Given the fact that India is a net exporter of talent and even the largest multinationals in India are staffed by Indian talent instead of expatriates, for investors in India, learning to deal with Indians is an inevitability they have to come to terms with relatively quickly. Those investors who are able to understand the motivations and aspirations of their counterparts and align their outcomes with those of their counterparts are likely to do much better over time than those who do not.

The risk appetite of Indian entrepreneurs and businesspeople has undergone major changes in recent decades. My father's generation had operated in an environment of scarcity in the 1970s and 1980s, when very little new wealth creation happened. He was brought up in an environment that used to emphasize protection of one's assets and that used to prescribe extreme risk aversion. As India opened up and started growing more rapidly, my generation experienced wealth creation during the 1990s and 2000s at a scale that could never have been imagined by the earlier generation. This wealth creation happened across sectors and was not the exclusive domain of endowed and wealthy individuals and families. First-generation entrepreneurs and technocrats built successful businesses in unusual fields and kindled the aspirations of many others. The risk appetite of Indian entrepreneurs and businesspeople has increased on average and the willingness to experiment with out-of-the-box and innovative ideas has increased as well.

Indian businesspeople have survived and prospered in a difficult and hostile business environment. They have dealt with many challenges, including those related to policy and governance, corruption, lack of infrastructure, tight liquidity, low productivity, and a culture of inefficiency all around. They have developed successful processes, practices, and business models to deal with these challenges. As they have grown in size and financial strength, they are now beginning to realize that almost all emerging and frontier markets face similar challenges. These businesspeople are now expanding their footprints into other emerging and frontier markets that have characteristics similar to India. The smartest and most agile of these entrepreneurs are likely to do very well and create a lot of wealth for themselves as well as for their partners and investors.

SUMMARY

Looking back, many mistakes were made in India by investors. Some were mistakes of their own commission and some others were the result of unpredictable changes in the Indian and global financial markets. Equities as an asset class have consolidated, and many of the mistakes of the past have either been buried or cleaned up. Equities are poised to benefit from any improvement in India's economy as well as its financial markets. Other asset classes are at various stages of consolidation and clean-up. They offer promise of future potential returns as India's economy and financial markets come around. However, their investment models will have to undergo significant changes. It has been proven beyond doubt that investment models of the previous decade do not work and that investors who wish to succeed will have to develop investment models that are more suited to India's on-the-ground realities.

Afterword

When I meet potential investors around the world and speak at investment conferences about India, the refrain that I consistently hear is "What is wrong with India?" When I talk about India's potential and the opportunities it presents, I am repeatedly asked why India has always been an unfulfilled promise and why it has consistently failed to deliver. I can understand their frustration and disappointment.

However, I do not agree that India has failed to deliver. India has produced consistently higher standards of living for its citizens since the onset of economic liberalization. The problem has been with the expectations of observers and investors alike and the comparison with economies like China that have followed a completely different developmental model.

I do concede that investors have not been rewarded for participating in the India opportunity during the past decade. However, in the case of investment returns, I compare India to the bamboo plant. The bamboo plant is one of the slowest-growing as well as one of the fastest-growing plant species in the world. For the first four years of its life, the bamboo plant does virtually nothing above ground. It requires fertile soil, water, and a conducive environment and grows underground building its root system and foundation. It can frustrate many a casual observer and can easily be written off as a failure. In its fifth year, the bamboo plant suddenly springs out of the ground and grows 80 feet in just six weeks, making it one of the fastest-growing plant species in the world. I think India will surprise investors who endure the frustration and stay the course.

When I take a look at the world today, there are very few places that have what India has going for it. India has a young and large population that is upwardly mobile. It is a country that is rich in human capital and has among the most talented populations in the world. It has democracy, rule of law, and protection of individual property rights, notwithstanding poor enforcement. It is a country that does not depend on the growth of other countries for its own prosperity and is perhaps an engine that will drive the prosperity of other countries in the future. Developed countries like the United States, Europe, and Japan are saturated and are dealing with the aftermath of the fall of communism and the integration of 3 billion people into the free world. Until equilibrium in standards of living is achieved in the world, there is very little hope for meaningful growth from these countries. Commodity exporters like Australia, Canada, Brazil, Russia, South Africa, and Indonesia are excessively dependent on the growth in China and other emerging markets. Their reliance on volatile commodity markets for their own prosperity is likely to pose challenges going forward. China itself is a wild card and is living with several conflicts and contradictions that need to be resolved and will likely be resolved sooner rather than later.

I grew up in India, but I pursued my higher education in the United States. When I graduated from the Wharton School at the University of Pennsylvania, I had opportunities to live and work in the pleasant environment of the United States like all my peers. I took a view for the next 30 years and decided that I wanted to relocate back to India. India has changed dramatically in the past 15 years and is likely to change even more in the next 15 years. The opportunity is to invest in that transformation.

The future is always unknown. An investor lays out money today in the "hope" of getting more of it back in the future. I have seen investors and analysts take a great deal of comfort in their Excel models and their research. Excel models can only set expectations of the future based on assumptions and cannot predict the future. One cannot research the future; by definition, research can be only of the past. Therefore, investing by itself is an act of optimism and I am an optimist. Optimism has not always helped me and has sometimes hurt me, but living with optimism is much better than living with pessimism.

I am a believer in the upward mobility of humans. One sixth of all humans in the world live in India, and they are at a very low base. Technology and communication have brought the world into their homes, and they now want to converge with the rest of the world. Skeptics, both from within the country and from overseas, often tell me that India's political system and governance is such a mess and corruption in India is so high that nothing will ever become of the country. If anything, they believe that the country will get worse and eventually fall apart. Obviously, I disagree with them. Indians might be poor and illiterate, but they know what they want and they are empowered with democracy that works. Democracies and free markets are both prone to periods of spectacular excesses and collapses but are self-correcting in nature. Democracies and markets both thrive on the new. Eventually, the mistakes of the past are buried and life moves on to creating the new. One might fret about the lost decade under the rule of the Congress Party and the leadership of Prime Minister Manmohan Singh. I prefer not to dwell on the past and instead to focus on the possibilities that lie ahead. Sentiment about India today is much worse than the reality in India. India is like an adolescent that is underconfident about itself and that does not inspire confidence about itself in others. Sentiment and confidence go in cycles just like businesses, economies, and financial markets. Sentiment toward India will come around and then commentators will once again talk about the very strengths of India that I've mentioned above.

India is a hardship posting today. It is an unpleasant country to visit and a frustrating one to work with. It has changed over the years and continues to change incrementally in a positive direction. The journey from where India is today to where it is needs to be tomorrow makes it one of the biggest untapped investment opportunities in the world.

About the Companion Web Site

This book includes a companion web site, which can be found at www.wiley .com/go/saraogiinvesting. The companion web site contains materials related to the case studies in the book including company annual reports, charts, and recommended web sites for articles and additional information. Following is a list of the companies discussed in the case studies:

Chapter 1:
Reliance Industries Limited
Tata Motors Limited
Ranbaxy Laboratories Limited
Chapter 2:
Coal India Limited
Jaiprakash Associates Limited
Chapter 3:
National Mineral Development Corporation
Chapter 4:
Kotak Mahindra Bank Limited
Sahara India
SKS Microfinance Limited
CRISIL Limited
Chapter 5:
Mahindra & Mahindra
Unitech Limited
Himatsingka Seide Limited
Bajaj Holdings
EID Parry India Limited
Godrej Consumer Products Limited

Godrej Properties Limited

Gujarat State Fertilizers and Chemicals

Chapter 6:

Gokaldas Exports Limited

Shriram Transport Finance Limited

To access the site, go to www.wiley.com/go/saraogiinvesting (password: india).

About the Author

RAHUL SARAOGI is the managing director of Atyant Capital Advisors, which advises the Atyant Capital family of funds for their investments in India. Rahul graduated from the Wharton School at the University of Pennsylvania. Rahul is one of India's leading value investors and has spoken at leading value investment conferences like Value Investing Congress in Pasadena and New York, Value Investing Seminar in Italy, ValueX in Zurich and Mumbai, and IQPC and Terrapinn conferences in Hong Kong and Singapore about investing in India. He has been featured on CNBC Asia as well as in publications like *The Manual of Ideas, The Value Investing Letter,* and *True Wealth.*

Rahul practices Vipassana meditation, which is a 2,500-year-old meditation technique rediscovered and taught by Gautama the Buddha. He believes that the biggest challenge investors face is their inability to deal with their own emotions of fear and hope and that Vipassana can help investors increase their equanimity to see things as they really are.

Rahul is an avid blogger on his web site www.atyantcapital.com. You can e-mail him at info@atyantcapital.com or follow him on Twitter @RahulSaraogi.

Rahul lives in Chennai, India, with his wife, Ruchita, and their four-year-old daughter, Miraya.

Index

Printed and bound by CPI Group (UK) Ltd, Croydon, CR0 4YY

15/01/2025

14626900-0005